John—
Ya inspire!!
Me Everyday!!
you are an amazing
Lecia

LEADERSHIP
LESSONS
FROM THE ROAD

FREE Downloads And Other Fun Stuff

Available At

www.NuckinFutz.com

Amy Morgan and Dr Wayne Pernell

LEADERSHIP LESSONS
FROM THE ROAD

Why Bother, We're All Nuckin' Futz!

ISBN: 978-0-9981461-3-3(sc)
ISBN: 97809-9981451-1-9(e)

Additional books may be ordered through book sellers or by contacting the authors via the contact form found at www.NuckinFutz.com

Because of the dynamic nature of the Internet, web addresses or links contained in this book may have changed since publication and may no longer be valid. Please start at www.NuckinFutz.com and/or reach out to either author via other social media platforms.

The authors of this book do not dispense medical, legal, or psychological advice, nor do they suggest any technique as a form of treatment for medical, physical, or emotional problems. Always consult the appropriate professional. The intent of the authors is solely to provide information of a general nature to aid the reader in attaining a greater perspective for personal and professional growth. No guarantees of growth are implied or promised. Your use of the information in this book for yourself and your actions are your responsibility and the author assumes no responsibility or liability for the outcome of those actions.

Printed in the United States of America

Release Date: 06/01/2018

Dedications

From Amy:

> To my husband Geoff Morgan who has lovingly (and not so patiently) taught me to accept that my way, isn't always the right way (I'm still working on that one).
>
> And to my daughters Rebecca and Caitlyn who have loved me from moment one, even if I am Nuckin' Futz!

From Wayne:

> Again, Shannon, my wife and my muse, has seen me through the Nuckin' Futz moments of another #1 Best-Selling book. Thank you for understanding that *this stuff must come out of me*. Thank you for recognizing that while the time and attention we take for our projects is time taken separately, it somehow allows us to be better for each other together.

Acknowledgments

Serving the legacy of Dr. Jim Pride has been an honor for us! His leadership and commitment to the Dental Community lives on through those he has inspired throughout the years.

We are also grateful for each of the team members we work with and all of the clients we support. There is no better feeling than knowing that we are surrounded by like-minded people who want to better themselves and others, and truly desire to significantly impact the lives of those they touch!

Foreword

The concepts for *Leadership Lessons From The Road* were drawn from real-life scenarios we, as consultants, have encountered on the road. That is, they came from you. We've seen it, and we've heard the call for "clean up on aisle 12." The truth is, running a dental practice is messy. Running any small business is messy.

It is also hugely rewarding. We love that you do what you do. It's also why we love what we do. Because ultimately, you create whole health in a circle that extends beyond the life you touch.

When we consult, we do the same. We're helping you help your patients or clientele, your teammates, the community, and even your family. In fact, as you read this, please think about how these concepts extend beyond the team. This book is for you, not as a business owner or a team member. This book, Leadership Lessons From The Road, is for you as a human.

So pay attention. This book will change your life if you let it. It might make you giggle at the absurdity of some situations, or it might make you cringe at the recognition of yourself. Either way, what you do with what is presented will make a difference in your life and in the lives of those you touch. Since our Vision is to positively impact the lives of all we touch, we extend you some happy reading and some potential growth.

Oh, and this was pretty cathartic for us as well. I mean, given all we've seen, we couldn't hold it in any longer. The names were changed to protect... well, you know who you are...!

Read on, enjoy, and be better for it.

Much Love,

Amy Morgan, CEO Pride Institute

Dr Wayne Pernell, Director of Organization Development, Pride Institute

Table of Contents

What is REAL Leadership and More Important, Why Bother...?

Amy's side:

I truly believe that true, authentic Leadership is needed now more than ever before! And, let's face it—all you have to do is whisper the word leadership, and many go running for the hills!

Why is leadership such a bitter pill to swallow? Trust me... I teach this and live this, and I definitely struggle with leading my own team, my clients, and don't even ask me how I'm doing with my kids! When I first came to work at Pride, I was young, brash (and unwrinkled) and because I'm from NY, I believed that leadership was fluffy and intangible, kinda granola-eating California stuff... all the empty gestures and slogans like "there is no I in team" rang untrue to me. I mean, at the time my favorite leadership statement was... "Do this or I'll kill you."

And then I met Dr. Pride... I will never forget our first deep conversation. I was chattering on about spreadsheets and my dismay at dental practice owners not understanding their numbers. At 6 ft 27 inches, he looked down on me from on-high and said, "Little girl (slightly politically incorrect, but I would pay someone to call me little girl now) ... little girl, it's Leadership, and it will always be Leadership!"

And that's how I began my lifelong journey of leadership lessons on the road. In coaching small business owners who struggle with these concepts even more than I did, I've seen the best of the best and unfortunately the worst of the worst. The worst includes running away from the concepts of leadership altogether (leaving teams with no direction at all) or thinking they have to behave like the wizard of Oz behind the curtain, trying to always be right, all knowing, all mighty and powerful (which leaves the team powerless, with no choice).

Neither is true nor effective. The challenge of leadership is how to truly communicate in a genuine way that connects with the hearts and minds of those who follow you. By sharing our Nuckin' Fitz Nuggets (disastrous leadership stories we have accumulated over the years) Wayne and I hope to accomplish One Small Leadership Step for Mankind. You can get all of the NF Nuggets at www.NuckinFutz.com. Hearing from two different leadership coaches' perspectives will help to cement the concepts that are universal – no matter the personality, the methods or the results. Believe me, WE HAVE SEEN IT ALL!

Grasshoppers (we are now your leadership senseis), learn from the dead carcasses of those leaders who have gone before you. Why? You, your team, your clients and your community deserve the opportunity to be inspired! Enjoy the journey, because although we are all NUCKIN' FUTZ... there is hope we can all be better!

= = = = = =

Wayne's side:

Very, very rarely does a team member awaken with an evil glint in his/her eye, a wry smile forming, and an exuberant exclamation that today is the day to really mess with (insert *your* name here). Yes, there are days that it feels like that. It feels like your team members are out to get you. It feels like the failing compressor is out to get you. It feels like your car is out to get you. Heck, the dog seems like he's out to get you, too.

And yet, you persist. And you might not even know why you do. But Amy and I know why you keep showing up and you didn't choose to shut the whole thing down. It's because you love it. You know, deep down, that what you offer to your clientele is valuable and potentially life changing. You know that you need to be there because they're counting on you. And while you hope that your team members will behave while you get ready to fire the lot of them, there's a part of you that loves that they keep showing up, too.

Leadership is a lot like parenting. You are being watched... All... The... Time!!! You're being watched, and what you say needs to be congruent with how you act. A message like "do what I say not what I do" isn't good for parenting, and it makes you a less-than-credible leader. Your team wants you to show up as someone who is positive and focused. Your team wants you to pave the way and to set boundaries. Your team wants you to communicate.

And all of this can be found in the pages that follow. Leadership is a labor of love. And this book is a tribute— okay, so it's a sideways tribute with a smirk— to that labor and that love. Really, this book came about as a labor of love, as well. Amy and I have different styles and we complement each other really well (Hey, nice shoes, Amy).

You're here to take a voyeuristic peek at the troubles of others hoping that what we've written isn't about you. The thing is, you've probably lived through it or seen it. And now, you're ready to get better. We all are.

Read on. Then, reflect—think about how you would handle things differently based on what you now know. Research— go to www.NuckinFutz.com and get more information, self-assessments, NF Nuggets, and more! Respond—yes, respond in multiple ways. We want to hear how you're doing. We want to hear what other questions you have. And we want to hear how you are showing up responsively for your team vs. reactively, as it may have been before.

Good luck to you, dear leader. You've got this.

And just remember: These really are leadership lessons from the road that just serve to underscore that we're _all_ just a little Nuckin' Futz!

Enjoy!

CHAPTER 1

It Starts and Ends with Vision – (You've Got To See the Forest through the Trees)

Amy: So, Wayne, I can't imagine any serious treatment of leadership _not_ starting with vision! That's amazing coming out of my mouth, considering I thought vision was so damn fluffy, but I am a vision convert. I don't believe that you can get anywhere in building a culture without a vision first. The vision is the plug that holds your bathtub water in. Without the plug, it creates a vortex that sucks the symbolic water - aka your energy, your resources and your results, right back down the drain!

Wayne: Right. Everybody needs to know where they're headed, and the vision needs to be based on something, right? It's one thing to say you have a vision, and it sort of sounds and feels like this vapor that's enveloping everybody. You waft it out there and hope everybody sees it, feels it, and responds to it. The vision has to be real, to be truly three dimensional, and for that to happen, it needs to be based on your current values! You need to really know what those values are for yourself and how to put those forward for your team in a way that inspires. We'll talk about communication in a bit. For now, we need to focus on what you're communicating. That's the "why" of it all. Your vision serves as a giant foundational anchor for you, the team, your clientele, your vendors and beyond!

Amy: If there's any nugget that we could share immediately, it's that

 **NUCKIN' FUTZ NUGGET:** whether you're talking about training a team member, deciding to expand your business, bringing on associates ... pretty much anything has to start with the *why* before you ever, ever approach the *how*.

And from my viewpoint, that "why" had better be compelling and truly desirable, because like the biblical story of Moses and the Jews who wandered through the desert for years and years and years, the only thing that kept them going for all that time (from a leadership perspective) was the fact that there was a pretty realistic/desirable *why* at the end of that trek, compelling generations to move forward!

Wayne: A great vision <u>does</u> provide the reason to get up in the morning. It provides a reason for both the leader as well as each team member. That's where the big "why" comes in. I think it's important to reflect on this as a business owner and as a human in the world: "What am I doing and why is that important?"

Ultimately, you're seeking the understanding of what drives you. It's why that "why" is so important. It goes beyond the idea that "we do what we do because we're going to make money," although that could be part of it. Profit *could* be *part* of a vision, but certainly it's about so much more! It's about service, community, relationships and it's about... wait for it ... your core values.

NUCKIN' FUTZ NUGGET: Take a minute, take a breather and think about this: What's your big why? What gets you out of bed in the morning? And then, lock that in a little bit. Every leader and every individual within a team needs to understand what their personal vision is, to see how it aligns with what the company's vision is, and be able to truly say "I believe in that!"

Amy: Exactly, because what gets you out of bed in the morning cannot be an "eat your spinach, shoulda-oughta-must" drudgery. What inspires you out of bed in the morning? What gets you doing the good, the easy and the hard stuff every day is a true belief that there is a compelling reason beyond the activity itself.

I know that you and I both agree that a vision has to be inspirational and aspirational, but I always add the third word, perspirational. If you are not humbled by the hard work and growth it may take to get to your "North Star" vision, then you're not dreaming big enough or broad enough. It's not going to get you out of bed, time after time after time.

Wayne: Let's talk about those three words because I think it's important to dive in a little deeper here.

Inspirational is something that when people (in general) think about this thing called *Vision*, they think that it's only purpose is to inspire—it serves to get you going. It may seem very fluffy and very far away, and may or may not be relatable. And really, that's not going to be a truly effective vision.

A true vision that's inspirational is more than just a platitude. A true vision is going to be something that really does serve to attach to the heart of every individual, while serving to pull each individual further forward toward what is possible.

Amy: If we look at the derivation of the word, it literally means to breathe life into something. In business it could mean to breathe life into the dead carcass of a plan, a protocol, a system, or the business itself. And so you're absolutely right, it has to be something that truly, truly creates motion in your ocean.

What about the word aspiration?

Wayne: **Aspirational** refers to something to aim for. Most people, when they write vision statements, will write things that they're already good at. And that's lovely, and you can pay tribute to that, but that's not part of a vision. An aspirational statement is something that is always on the horizon. You may be good at what you do, and a true vision can honor that and say there is always room to get better, be better, and have better.

Amy: One of our clients, Dr. Ben Jameson, used to explain aspirational in this way: his brother is a well-known painter, and one day when Ben was in his studio, he admired a beautiful landscape painting. Ben went over to his brother and said, "That's beautiful. Have you been there?" And his brother's response was, "Not yet, but someday I will."

Wayne: Nice.

Amy: And that, to me, represents aspirational. And of course my favorite word is **perspirational**. You know, you have to roll up your sleeves and make your vision a reality. The empty vision is what I call this the "Miss America" vision. The "I want to help all the little children of the world, while I'm wearing this bikini and high heels and can't spell the words world or peace."

If I had a nickel for every mission statement I've ever seen that says we're a quality practice, or a quality business here to serve ... I'd be retired in Tahiti, and the heck with this book and to heck with my life's calling as a business consultant.

The perspirational means that you've got to DO, TO MAKE IT HAPPEN. Yes it's the horizon, and yes the horizon is always going to be three, four, five steps ahead of you. But it's the motion in the ocean that we're looking for, which means it's always going to be hard— but deeply worth it.

Wayne: Yes Amy! The vision, to play off of the Miss America kind of thing, is if you look in a phone book— if you remember phone books, the Yellow Pages...

Amy: O-M-G, you are so old, Wayne. Yes, we'll try, for our reader's sake.

Wayne: So, way back in the olden days, the idea was that if you looked in a phone book under "plumber," for example, you would see just about every single plumber listed as "honest plumber." And that became a joke because no one says, "Well let me keep looking in this phone book for a dishonest one." It's the bland, "I'm not-so-uniquely wonderful for you" statement.

NUCKIN' FUTZ NUGGET: So really, the idea here is that these three words—inspirational, aspirational and perspirational—are about building on the foundation that moves your business forward. Your vision does serve to be *inspirational*, it serves to breathe life back into your plan, your true desires, which are values based, by the way. Then *aspirational*, that you're moving toward something bigger, grander than what you have and are right now. And the *perspirational* part is that there is work to be done to move toward that North Star. What is the work that you're going to do?

Now, a vision statement doesn't have to be, "Step one: I will wake up. Step two: I will get dressed. Step three: I may brush my teeth. Step four ..." It's not that. It is talking about specifically, and generally, the steps you will take to move toward your ideal state. How will you rally your troops? How will you serve your customers? In what way?

And all of that combined — the inspirational, aspirational, and perspirational — does lead you to something that should serve to get you up in the morning, and should serve to ... you know, the way I see it, it's like a banner of your values and beliefs that you plant at the top of a hill when you boldly shout out, "Follow me!"

Amy: Exactly. And just one more point: A vision can't inspire others, until it truly inspires the leader. Which means you can't fake it till you make it. There's nothing worse than waking up and going, *"Oh my god. I'm working for the man."* And then realizing the man is you. *"I hate my boss. Wait a minute — that's me."* That's a real sign that you're serving a false vision, or a vision that no longer serves your values or your current circumstances.

NUCKIN' FUTZ NUGGET: It's not a burden if it actually is a North Star that you truly desire. The perspiration is worth it if you desire it. And so, for any leader who has ever suffered the pain and itch of burn-out, the first step you need to take to solve that is re-discover, *"What is my North Star?"* and *"How do I recalibrate my business to actually line up to the motion in the ocean to achieve that North Star?"*

Wayne: That is a great point! Let's talk for a minute about how you find your North Star. One of the key things for any work we do with leaders, is to always starts with values. "What do you value? And what do you hold as something that, if it was taken from you, would cause you to suffer?" Is this value-based thing about freedom? Is this value of family? Is this value tied to spirit, for example? If any of those were taken from me, yes, I would suffer. So, those things need to be built into the vision… the Values-Based Vision.

Amy: Absolutely. And I like to make the distinction with my clients, and I know you do the same, that I believe each one of us comes to our life's purpose with core values. Those core values, whether you want to argue nature or nurture, they're permanent. Aside from a lobotomy or years of coma, those core values are going to remain the same. And you can count on that. You have to trust that your core values are set, because I do believe that business values shift.

That's one of the ways in which people begin to not be inspired by their vision statement, is that if you don't notice the shift, then you are soon serving a vision that is no longer relevant! For example, when you first opened your practice, your business, yes, profitability had to be a key business value. Absolutely. Twenty years in, your retirement is fully funded, your business is successful. Now, you want your kids to know you as more than a shadow figure that shows up every now and then on their soccer field to watch a game. Your value, as far as a business value, has shifted, and you need to make sure that your foundational business is serving those shifting values, trusting that your core values will never lead you down an evil path.

Wayne: **NUCKIN' FUTZ NUGGET: It's a huge distinction and one that's really important to make: There is a difference between personal core values and business values. That is conceptually something that gets confused at times. The bottom line here is that it is OK for vision to change, understanding that your core values probably don't.**

In your example, Amy, you talked about going to see the child on the soccer field. Absolutely right. The core value there is family. Twenty years ago, did the business value of profitability serve the core value of family? Yes. Does the business value of more time off for self and others serve the personal value, the core value, of family? Yes, the core value hasn't changed. So, I think that's really an important distinction to make and to highlight.

Amy: Well that's why sometimes it does feel like working for the man. *"Boy, I have to work. I can't take any time off because my boss will be mad at me. Wait…I'm the boss, right? Yes I can. And I never signed an agreement that I had to be at my business eight hours a day, five, six, seven days a week."*

It is very important to make sure that as you're drawing the line in the sand as to _why_ you go to work every day, and if you expect others to be inspired by it, physician heal thyself. Look in the mirror and make sure that it does inspire you, which means it delivers on something that you value that's really important to you.

I know I have tons of "what-not-to-do's" from my leadership lessons from the road, and I know that you do, too. So, shall we hop into that?

Wayne: Great idea! Let's hop!

My first "What not to do" is: "Do this because I said so." That is a really strong leadership statement that is just so misguided (and paternal or militaristic) and will basically drive your business, and your team's morale, into the ground. It is one of the mistakes that people make when they think that they are "supposed to" be the boss that acts bossy, and whatever else the role of the boss is. Demanding, commanding as the one-note of leadership, is not leadership.

Amy: Absolutely. A vision statement is not a communist propaganda song that everybody sings in perfect unison. My viewpoint is, it's not the recitation of the vision, it's the living it, every day! I recently was in an office for an "intervention." Neither the practice owners nor the team were on the same page. In fact, there were factions, or gangs, representing their own silos of special interests. The confidential team surveys revealed a completely toxic environment. My favorite quote was, *"It's bad here.... But I used to work for Enron."* Once I got the owner/leaders to begin to look in the mirror, they realized they could no longer band together under the same vision they established 10-plus years ago. Even though the whole team could quote the vision verbatim, and every morning huddle would end with the recitation of that vision—nobody was living it! Why? Because, nobody wanted to live it, as it no longer represented their vision, their values, nor their brand identity.

To take a step back into positive territory, we had the owners present their realizations to their very unhappy, divided team in an effort to get everyone back on the same page. At the end of their meeting, they all decided to burn their old vision statement in effigy. Everybody had a match, and everybody had to state a personal commitment to re-group before they set it on fire. I admit the symbolic imagery was a little drastic, but it did the trick!

NUCKIN' FUTZ NUGGET: Although we want that vision to be a unifier for a business, the true purpose of the vision statement is to be the "mothership." Synergy comes from finding team members who have, whether they're aware of it or not—we all have it—

personal vision and who see the mothership as a vehicle to accomplish their own vision. Win-Win!

And that's where synergy comes into play. *"I see your why; this is my why. If I put my energy toward achieving your why, it's going to take my why down the road, as well. Yippee-ki-yay, let's do this."*

Wayne: These are huge, huge points worth underscoring. One is, it may be that the team can recite the vision, but if it means nothing, it's just like a nursery rhyme. And this is something that we see in organizations a lot. This really happens all the time! All the team members gather around and recite the vision, just because it's a vision and it's the thing to do. Unfortunately, all that noise is just another meaningless morning exercise. The Vision is something that really needs to be lived into.

Another one of the mistakes that some leaders make is that they don't leave room for each individual team member to have their own vision. And so, it really is important that the individual visions be acknowledged with the overarching, as you say, "mothership" to be *the* vision that everyone lives into.

Amy: Absolutely. The running joke that I always go back to is that future dental assistants very rarely ever looked up at the sky in third grade and said, *"Dear*

Lord someday I want to suck spit for a dentist and make his or her life miserable." Right? They wanted to be astronauts and ballerinas, and as they get older, they want to be moms and dads who actually earn a great living so that their kids can have the lifestyle they want, or they have many other pressing needs and desires.

The bottom line is that if you want a passionate team, you can't just pump in the passion one way. Passion needs to go two ways! Think about any business you've ever seen that has a strong team who act as ambassadors to the vision. You need to know they're inspired ambassadors because they not only support the owner's vision, they also believe this mothership will accomplish their own dreams. And you can't fake this.

Wayne: It's true. It's interesting to think about the culture of today. People want it all. Instead of saying, "Oh I want to be a ballerina," or "Gosh, I want to be an astronaut," these days it's not unusual for any of us, no matter what our age at this point, to say I want to be both. I want to be this **_and_** that, *and* that, *and* that. And there's no reason why not, unless the elective choices turn into distractions and pull away from the main vision.

Amy: Another mistake we all see in our clients is,

NUCKIN' FUTZ NUGGET: Yes, we now all agree that the Why is almighty, all powerful. It is the plug that holds your business' bathtub water in. But without the How, it's empty rhetoric.

It's the New Year's resolution 'I want to lose 25 pounds while I eat this quart of ice cream and hang out on the couch.' At some point you have to actually have the exercise and diet plan in place. The good old' standby slogan, "A leader has to walk their talk," applies here. The why (vision), represents the talk, and the how (strategy/action) is the walk. You, dear leader, have to dare to dream, and you also have to dare to strategize so that the dream becomes a reality. And honestly, when we walk into offices where credibility is the number one issue—where every time the doctor says something, team members react with an eye-roll—it's apparent it comes from the cynicism that stems from too much why and not enough, or any, how.

Wayne: Exactly! If you are going to rally the team with a promise of a better tomorrow, you had better have a roadmap to achieve it. You can only promise a promised land, a better tomorrow, so many times. The leader then has to deliver.

NUCKIN' FUTZ NUGGET: One of the things that I like to do with my clients is to ask them to rank themselves on the vision at the end of the day. Did I live into it? On a scale of 1 to 10, did I do this thing I said I'd do? Did I do *this* thing I said I'd do? Did I do <u>*this*</u> thing I said I would do?

Those are huge questions at the end of the day, and that does speak to the how. Because the why gets you moving, the how needs to be consistent, and it needs to be flexible—and those, by the way, are huge traits of leaders that we'll talk about a little bit in a while, in another section of this book: the concepts of credibility and flexibility.

Amy: You're absolutely right. The bottom line is that if you do it right, just like you said, rate yourself, the vision can be the third person in the room with you always.

What brings your vision to life is:

- If you're deciding that you want to acknowledge a team member, you're acknowledging them through the vision.

- If you're counseling a team member, you're counseling them through the vision.

- If you're hiring, you're hiring through the vision.

- If you're purchasing, you're purchasing to the vision.

- If you're adapting, continuously improving, you're adapting to the vision.

    So, when it is the third person in the room, it gives that vision the heft it needs. It's no longer empty, fluffy, or a slogan just to be repeated and thrown away. To the degree it becomes a part of every aspect of your business life is the degree that the vision will work for you.

Wayne:

NUCKIN' FUTZ NUGGET: One of the things that we say is that the vision acts as the lens through which all decisions are made. And that means action is taken only when filtered by, "does this match our vision?"

That, in itself, is pretty gigantic. Because if you knew that your core values were tied to every action step, and you were conscious of that, just imagine how your day would go. And this is where a lot of leaders lose the energy that drives them; it's when they forget what their core values are, and they forget that every action step needs to be made *consciously* through that filter.

Then you've got a gigantic pathway—a broad pathway, significant pathway—to which you can guide your team. More important, guide yourself.

Amy: You know, Wayne, another observation of a Nuckin' Futz moment on the road is business leaders, with the fear of scarcity, who write their vision more like an advertising slogan. Their fear is that if they put their needs and desires into a North Star, they won't be able to share this because

"My patients, or my customers, or my vendors, or my community may not buy into it." "I need my vision to please my potential new patients, more than fulfill me."

Wayne: Can you *dare* to be great?

Amy: Can you dare to be great? Can you dare to dream? Because we all know, no guts, no glory. This is your vision, not an advertising slogan like "World's best cup of coffee"! It's more than just saying "we're open Saturdays and weekends, and here to serve our patients, and accept any and all insurance plans and heavily discount...." which is all very one-sided. If you're getting nothing in return, then you might as well be a not-for-profit charity. Own the fact that this is a for-profit business vision based on someone with core values that are ethical and honest.

Wayne: Yeah! We talk about daring to be great, and we talk about the consistency or congruence of 'world's best cup of coffee.' And so what if it is dentistry? What if it is business leadership? What if it is whatever business it is—this primarily is for our dental teams. What do you dare to say?

High tech? Comfortable? Cottage-based? Who are you? And what do you value? And what will you never be? And those are the things that really need to be thought about and expressed. We've seen leaders who basically live and work out in the middle of nowhere, and they tout themselves as being the highest tech and finest. And while the service they provide is great, the "vibe" of the practice would be better described as country. When the disparity is there, and it's such a mismatch, credibility is shot.

Even when they have great technology, it's such a mismatch for the culture that they're trying to build. I think that's a huge distinction as well, is that *your vision really needs to speak to the culture you want to build. (That's a little mini-NF Nugget right there!)*

Amy: Absolutely. The other point that I see that traditional mission statements or purpose statements only focused on, is what the practice provides to their patients/what a business uniquely promises to give to their consumer. And just like the concept of the "world's best cup of joe," you create a relationship that gives and gives and gives, with no expected return! And (I'm allowed to say this because I have one waiting for my phone call as we speak), no Jewish-mother visioning. The *"It's okay I'll sit in the* *dark. I'm here for my kids."* And we all know that is not just the stereotype of the Jewish mother— it's any mother that smothers with guilt. How that translates in the dental office is, "we provide tremendous clinical outcomes, an amazing experience and on-going support, and we expect nothing in return! Relationship-oriented businesses have to build on the premise that all interactions are win-win, *"I give you this and I expect this in return."*

So if your vision is to deliver ideal care utilizing the finest technology, then in exchange, your ideal patient truly values that technology and results, delivered in a relationship-oriented, personal-touch environment. They demonstrate their value, by partnering in their commitment to long-term health, becoming ambassadors of the practice.

So there's always a yin to a yang, which makes you feel like there's a two-way flow versus a one-way flow, which can be energy sapping versus energy fulfilling.

Wayne: So true, Amy, because if you've got a vision that says, "We give and give and give and give and give and give," there's no *you* left.

NUCKIN' FUTZ NUGGET: One of the things that I think is so important to remember is that *you can't give what you don't have.*

When you've run out of fuel because you've given everything you have, there's nothing left to give.

The ideal vision needs to communicate that we are here to serve the people that are here to receive, thrive, and engage with us. I think that is a huge distinction for success.

Amy: Absolutely.

And of course we know that part of the win-win relationships needed to forward the vision is how to get and keep the team involved. One of the biggest mistakes that I see that our clients make is when they only trot out their vision statement to correct a non-performing team member or to bring up a mistake.

Wayne: Yes, "the rolled-up newspaper."

Amy: Yes, exactly. If that "rolled-up newspaper in puppy training" vision statement is only trotted out when the "puppies piddle on the carpet", your "puppies" aren't going to buy into the vision for the long haul, even if they saw it as the mothership at first! They may fear the vision statement as it represents "the stick"—the potential negative consequence—but they're not going to be inspired by it.

NUCKIN' FUTZ NUGGET: So again, going all the way back to your vision being a filter, as the third person in the room with you, to base your successful culture on the vision: You need to use it to catch your patients / clients, and your team doing things right, almost right, or not completely wrong, and acknowledge it. Appreciate it, value it, and grow it through the inspiring lens of the vision.

Once you have that in place, when there is something to correct it might not even have to be said, because your team will know that their role in creating and maintaining a self-sustaining, self-correcting environment is the path to success and the path to achieving the vision. And if I'm parked on the side of that path, that vision is either going to compel me back on the path or compel me off the path altogether.

Wayne: Yes absolutely. In personal development as well as professional development, we know that *you get more of what you focus on*. So if you're focusing on the negative, you're likely to see more of the negative. If you're focusing on what's working, you're likely to see more of that.

The way that we talked about doing the personal vision assessment at the end of the day—*"Did I live into the vision on a scale of 1 to 10"*—the same has to be true for what you do with your team. *"Did I live up to my vision in supporting my team?"* and *"Did each individual team member support, promote and personify my vision through their actions today?"* Every team meeting (I hope you're having team meetings—more on that in chapter 5) has to have a focus on how we lived into the vision. Not a focus on did we? But actually, *how* did we? It's really a matter of getting every team member's engagement around how we do this, hourly, daily, weekly and beyond; what worked for us, and how do we do more of that?

This ties to a leader not knowing how to bring the vision to the team, to bring it to life at the beginning, the middle and at transition.

The gentleman that I have in mind is adorable, and very ... he's sort of a perfectionist, and he doesn't want to bring his vision to the team because he doesn't know that the team that's in place is going to be the one that's in place six months from now, or a year from now—so he's not sure how to bring his vision to them. And the response is, or the next tactical step is: the only way to do it is to **do it**.

You've heard a major company use that slogan, and it really is a great slogan. It's got to be pronounced. You have to bring your vision out. You have to share it and let people know what you believe in. Remember, your vision is based on your core values. Even if it's a current business vision that you do modify in a year, or two years, or five years, if it's working for you, that's great. If it's not, fix it. But the first step is to bring it out and let people see it.

Amy: Absolutely, yes, because they're never going to believe the messenger if they don't know what the messenger believes in, and that's essential.

When you do bring it to the team, make sure you are not "selling." Just because it's printed on pretty paper, or just because it's in a frame on the wall of your reception area or in the staff lounge, or just because you hand it to somebody and say, "Read this", does not an inspiring vision statement make.

NUCKIN' FUTZ NUGGET: They have to hear your voice. They have to hear it. They have to watch your skin tone. They have to notice the inflection, the breathing, they need to see excitement or enthusiasm, to whatever degree. Because, trust me, none of you have to start sniffing glue in order to look super excited about your vision. You rise to the level of excitement that doesn't make you look like you've been abducted by aliens.

Wayne: I will say this, though, that it won't hurt to increase your level of excitement by 10% to 20%, because what you currently think of as excitement is not seen by your team as excitement. I can almost guarantee that. I know you look in the mirror when you brush your teeth. Try smiling and look in the mirror. Do your eyes smile? Does your mouth really show what you are feeling? Smile with excitement. Dare to spill out some love, too. (Yes, I said... love!)

Amy: Absolutely. So, rising to your highest level of passion is a good thing, because your vision is you. In a small business, your vision is you. And if you can't wear it, be it, embrace it, and walk hand-in-hand with it—if your team even sniffs that it's a hidden agenda or propaganda—from that point forward they're going to filter everything you say with a cynical tone or expectation, so if you want your vision to live, then live it. Live it. That's really important.

And then finally, you know Dr. Pride used to say when you find yourself on a dead horse, get off. I see business owners fall in love with their original line in the sand, their original business vision, and become incredibly hesitant to change one word, because somehow that negates what that vision represented to them in the first place.

We already gave everyone ample permission that as your business values shift, so does that horizon, that point B, that North Star. And when that happens, new words that actually support and promote that new goal are absolutely essential. You can use the original vision statement as the legacy vision statement, but you've got to move on, and the test for each leader is, *"When is it time for me to move on?"* Is there any motion in your ocean? If you're stuck, if you ain't moving, if you're lifeless, if your team is lifeless, or your new patient flow is lifeless… wink-wink, nudge-nudge. Get off that dead horse, find yourself a stallion and rock and roll.

Wayne: I have one caveat to that, Amy, and that is that the business vision isn't changed every two weeks just because there's no motion, right? Just because it *feels* dead.

 **Nuckin' Futz Nugget:** If it feels dead, Dear Leader, that's you. And that means that you have to really reflect on the energy that you're putting into your Vision and bringing to the team.

Wayne: It goes back to core values. These aren't made up. These are core values that you believe in. So, what do you believe in? And how can your core values be folded into the vision that you bring forward for your team, for your patients, your clients, your customers, even your vendors? Every decision you make has to be filtered, and preferably consciously, through the core values and through the vision.

Amy: So the key leaderships lessons, in summary, are as follows: *Number one, trust yourself.*

Wayne: Yes! And be trust-worthy by being authentic! Be genuine. Be real. Be YOU!

Amy: Again, if your core values are evil, then don't do a vision statement. Or do a really good evil vision statement, but trust yourself. We're going to assume you're good people who want to better yourselves and others. That's in *our* vision statement.

Wayne: Sure. We've referred to the North Star earlier. Assuming that people are "good people" and living that way, modeling the way as a person who is truly good is a great way of leading!

Amy: Trust yourself. Which means draw your line in the sand, and base everything you do on your core values and your ever-evolving business values. What's your next leadership lesson?

Wayne: Make it clear! Communicate (which we're going to get into in the next chapter or so). Communicate: What is it that you believe in? People have to know that, and they have to know that you believe in what you're saying. This is really a "walk the talk" kind of message. Communicate what it is you believe in, and certainly, don't assume that anyone will know that.

Amy: Make sure that you're comfortable with your role as the mothership, and leave plenty of room for your team to have their own personal vision, personal North Stars, and your job is to draw the synergistic connection between accomplishing your vision and the accomplishment, or at least the motion toward accomplishing, their vision.

Wayne: And I would say a homework assignment, something to think about that most leaders actually don't put time into, is to really contemplate these three simple (yet advanced) questions:

* What are you willing to do to support the vision?

*What are you willing to do for yourself, for your team, and for your clientele?

*What action steps do you need to take to inspire, aspire, and perspire?

And that could be buying something, that could be celebrating something, that could be advertising something, or it could be giving something away. What are you willing to do to show—to really demonstrate—that you are truly living the vision every day?

Amy: Because the bottom line is that maturity comes when you understand that a strong, clear, concise and inspirational aspirational vision is the foundation that you build all success for your business. And without it, it's a house of cards.

Wayne: Indeed.

Amy: Yippee-ki-yay.

CHAPTER 2

Nuckin' Futz - Communication... It Ain't Ever What You Say; It's How You Say It!

Amy: So Wayne, if we're writing a book about Leadership Lessons From The Road, why write a chapter about communication?

Wayne: Communication is the thread that weaves through everything!!!

Amy: Yes it is!   And nine times out of ten, when a system breaks down, it's because either internal communication (team to team, leader to team, team to leader) or external communication (team to customer, customer to team) has broken down!

Wayne: In fact, you and I just visited a large team where everyone agreed that communication (or lack thereof) was one of the major issues holding them back from going to the next level. Even though to us they all agreed it was a problem, no one could communicate the ramifications or the solutions directly to each other — a classic example of a Nuckin' Futz moment! I think one of the key things that makes communication such a hard thing to wrestle to the ground is the fact that if we asked every single team member we encounter what communication meant to them, we would get as many different answers as there are team members.

Amy: Absolutely! We know that effective leadership communication is the bridge between intention and realistic impact. Nobody is ever going to intend their way into inspiring somebody to do what you want them to do, so it's not just communication that's important. It's the *kind* of communication, because there are some definite Nuckin' Futz Nuggets that we can talk about! Bottom line: there is always some form of communication occurring, but very often it is the wrong kind of communication. Positive communication that actually inspires and influences, that promotes action, is the first of many leadership lessons necessary in order to create a culture of continuous growth, improvement and on-going success!

Wayne: So where do we start?

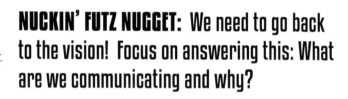

NUCKIN' FUTZ NUGGET: We need to go back to the vision! Focus on answering this: What are we communicating and why?

I think it always has to tie back to values. What are the core values that the business owner wants to

Write Core Values

communicate about? And how will those values be communicated? Team members and anyone who does business with you want to know who are you as a business owner. Who are you in the community? What do you want to make your practice be about and stand for? All of that has to be communicated in a way that people can hear it, see it, and touch it!

Amy: True, and of course, to quote one of my favorite books of all time, *The Leader's Voice*, "the difference between a vision and a hallucination is how many people see it."

Wayne: Right! So it's all in *how* it's communicated.

Amy: Exactly, because very often a leader, when they wake up in the middle of the night with a non-performing or unhappy team member dancing on their head, knows what their ideal vision is, what they want from that team member —but doesn't have the tools to be able to communicate it in a way that goes beyond the Peanuts teacher, wah, wah, wah, wah, wah.

So shall we talk about the dark side? Like, what have you seen? I mean, to me, there are three major missteps when it comes to Nuckin' Futz communication: over-communication, under-communication, and miscommunication.

Wayne: You know, I think an entire chapter can be written about miscommunication because it shows up in so many different ways. Let's talk about over-communication here. Because we're going to be talking about leadership in one of the next sections, and I think communication comes through as over-communication when it's also micromanaging. Do this... no, I said do this, this, this. This step, this step. So yeah, Amy, let's talk about over-communication.

Amy: Over-communication to me is death by too many words. The vomit-and-spew session where a leader explains his or her position, whether we're talking about a staff meeting or one-on-one, and then over-explains and then over-explains and then over-explains.

An example of that is very often leaders who are not comfortable with unnecessarily stirring the pot or handling conflict tend to hide the real issues, questions or desired outcomes.

NUCKIN' FUTZ NUGGET: It is essential for any leader of a team—large or small—to become comfortable with assertive communication! "Here's what I see, this is what I need, and what are your next steps to achieve a positive outcome?"

I once was sitting in with a doctor doing a counseling session with a less-than-stellar, poor performing team member. The hidden agenda was that the doctor really wanted to drop-kick that staff member through the goal post of life. My agenda was to give the team member the opportunity to understand the elements of her poor performance, the consequences of that continuing, and a choice to change. I coached the doctor to be very direct/assertive in her communication, practicing:

"I saw you _____. This can't continue because it violates our vision. I expect that this will be handled immediately if you want to continue to be part of the team"

And...here's how it came out.

"Sit down. You know what? I love working with you so much. You're such a joy and I love your family, and by the way, this can't continue, but I'm so happy you're on my team," and I was like, WHAT? That person just walked out of that meeting, I believe, thinking she just got a raise instead of having been confronted on an inappropriate behavior or result!

Wayne: Sure, it's been said that the meaning of a message is the response you get.

And when team members have a different meaning than the leader intended after speaking with that leader, that's a problem. I've seen where leaders have basically gone on a long soliloquy, a long, long monologue, and have basically said everything that they've been thinking about without having an agenda.

In doing that, the team members feel that they've been run over. They feel held hostage, and they don't feel like they've had a chance to contribute.

NUCKIN' FUTZ NUGGET: It is important to understand the differences between "push communication" versus "pull communication." There are times when you have information that must be disseminated quickly via "push communication"—push it out, spit it out, do it, and get the information that everybody needs out there. The problem is that there's no guarantee of it being heard as intended. So really, the remedy is to pull. Practice "pull communication," where you're asking questions to gain understanding and buy-in.

Amy: Agreed. Once you accept the idea that communication can be assertive without being obnoxious, the next thing to remember is that leadership is something you do <u>with</u> people, not <u>to</u> people. It is a dialogue, not a monologue, and certainly not a Shakespeare soliloquy. Then, third, is that if you've got a point, communicate the point and then shut up your face.

Wayne: Well, I have to concur. You know, over-communication often appears when there's a lack of confidence.

The insecure leader ends up feeling like he/she has to fill empty space. Often over-communication could be the equivalent of uh, you know, like, uh, when something could be said very quickly, very succinctly. We've all seen it. We've all experienced it.

So, I won't continue to talk, because that would be over-communicating.

☺

UNDER-COMMUNICATION

Wayne: Under-communication is one of my favorites. I think it bleeds over into miscommunication, and it shows up so often. I see it when business owners or doctors will have conversations with themselves in their head, and they will have played out the entire conversation of what they're going to say to a team member before they get to the office, and they come in, and it's almost as if they start the conversation with the team member with something like, "So, you're going to get that done, right?"

And that's the conversation, and the team member is left confused, wondering where all of that came from and what is needed to fix it and why all of a sudden?

Amy: Well, it's funny because I think saying *something* is at least halfway there. I've seen doctors try to just transmit their thoughts telepathically—without saying a word…

When I ask a doctor if he has had a conversation with a team member that is not performing a goal, task or skill up to par, it's not unusual to hear,

"Oh, she knows I'm upset."

How does she know?

"I didn't give her a cookie at lunch and I didn't say thank you at the end of the day."

In fact, the message that staff member probably received is that you are getting fat and hogging the extra cookies and that you're ungrateful! You have to say something, and you know, a lot of times leaders who aren't confident will have that conversation as you said, in their head, but actually never spit it out. The irony is that six weeks later, after many a Tylenol ingested, you could put that doctor on a lie detector they'd be absolutely certain that they had communicated to the person and the situation had been successfully handled!

Does it mack ง 5/01

Wayne: You know, there's a theme that comes up which is that these conversations are one-sided, right? Well, that conversation happened in his or her head on the drive in. The thinking then is that since it happened, the team member should know. Or it's again back to the term "push communication." It's one-sided without inviting conversation or without inviting input.

Amy: One of my favorite stories that our founder of Pride Institute, Dr. Jim Pride, would tell as he was teaching leadership, is that the very first staff member that he ever hired was a woman named Elaine, and she came to work the very first day to run his front desk dressed in full-tilt boogie nurse's gear, with the yellow pad, ready to be this amazing, stereotypical healthcare provider. Jim had been thinking all night long about what this first staff member was going to do and how wonderful she was going to be, and when he sat down with her that first day, she said, "What do you want me to do in my new position?" His response was, "Elaine, I want you to work." To which she replied, "How?" His response was, "Really hard."

To him, that communicated the wide scope and frame of what he was hoping that position could be. Now, working good and hard meant a great deal more to him than it did to Elaine, and of course that led him down a road of severe disappointment, and her down a road to not having a job for very long. That's a classic example to me of under-communication.

Wayne: Yep, yep. I think going back to telepathic communication—the whole idea of, well, they could tell I'm mad or they could tell that upset me. It's like, how could they tell? Well, I could tell that my face turned red. You know, so they know that means I'm mad.

Amy: No, they think you ate something bad for lunch.

Wayne: **NUCKIN' FUTZ NUGGET:** Under-communication demands a return back to your values and what's reflected in the vision. What part of the vision or what part of the values are not being carried forward that allow for you to feel good or bad about the way things are going?

Amy: So, to summarize: Use your mouth, exercise your vocal cords.

Know what you want to say, say it succinctly, but say it until you have some kind of a cue from the person you're saying it to that they actually heard and will respond in the way that you intended them to respond. That's a cure, from my viewpoint, of the telepathic under-communication or the one-word communication that doesn't truly match or mirror all that's going on inside your brain.

MISCOMMUNICATION

Wayne: There's over-communication, under-communication, and miscommunication! Let's dive into this last one.

Amy: You know, it's interesting—when you say miscommunication, it always reminds me that if I say the word orange, to one person it means a color, to another person it means a fruit, and to another person it's a county in California or Florida where it costs a lot of money to live.

NUCKIN' FUTZ NUGGET: What you think you're saying very often is not heard the way in which you would like it to be heard.

Two-way communication is required to make sure that there's no miscommunication, but boy, do we have a lot of sad stories of miscommunication through our leadership lessons from the road. Do you have any sweet ones?

Wayne: I think some of the scariest examples of miscommunication happen via text. It's the best of the worst miscommunication. "Well, I texted my team; they should know." Or the team texts, and the doctor responds, and, well, do you think that conveys exactly, _exactly_ what your real intention is?

Amy: Texting, email... we all know that one misplaced exclamation point in any kind of a written format without the body-mind-spirit being there denotes a totally different topic, which goes back to the point that communication has to be two-way.

Wayne: Exactly.

Amy: You know, I actually have an example, and I know that you've had this: One of the clients that we work with was always so afraid of setting goals.

Wayne: Yes! The fear is about actually having to achieve the goals that are set, right?

Amy: They're afraid because they're going to be perceived as production-driven versus serving their community in a quality, service-oriented and ethical way, and of course we know that setting the goal doesn't make you more production-driven. It actually takes away the scarcity and gives the team a real finish line to calibrate their efforts and intentions. Very often, the doctor—by not setting goals and constantly pestering the front-office team, "When's that next patient going to be scheduled?"—actually is now perceived more production-driven, because they're constantly trying to push for more.

So, it's not the communication of the goal that is the problem, but the perception of the team that all this dude's interested in is *more*. That's a classic example that we see time and time again.

Wayne: It's true. And really, it's the communication of _more_ what?

Amy: Right.

Wayne: Right? Because so often we get doctors that want more for the wrong reason. We get doctors that want to hit a production goal because there's some number in their head that is like a magic number for them, and so they're driven to this thing, and everything that they communicate is about this number, this number, this number, instead of what the meaning of the number actually is. Really, reflect on what the meaning of it actually is!

Amy: I also think that miscommunication can happen as a result of misdirection. A leader who does not understand the fine art of confrontation and conflict resolution will communicate really well to those that they feel most confident and comfortable communicating to. That brings communication through triangulation!

"If I tell my favorite, Mary, that I'm unhappy with Beth, then somehow I have fulfilled my responsibility, and Beth now knows I'm unhappy. Bonus - Mary will love me more."

But of course we know that the minute you have more than two staff members on your team, you are now playing the childhood game of operator. And what you communicate to Mary may be something about how she communicated to a patient on the telephone, and by the time it actually gets to Beth it could be something completely different.

NUCKIN' FUTZ NUGGET: Bottom line, be careful when you triangulate and start that good old telephone game, because you might start by saying you have failed, and in translation it might sound like you're fired. This will not win you any friends—nor address the change you desire!

OK, WE NOW KNOW WHAT NOT TO COMMUNICATE. WHAT ARE THE REMEDIES?

Wayne: So, under the heading of communication, I see that _styles_ of communication need to be addressed. What we know is that there are three styles that every leader needs to know that they are using:

- COMMAND

- CONSULTATIVE

- CONSENSUS

The <u>command</u> style of communication is a direct order. It is a level of expectation that is communicated clearly and succinctly, and it sounds like:

"The hygiene room needs to be turned over in this way."

"New Patients are to be scheduled in afternoon appointments."

"Everyone must be on time for our morning meeting and participate fully."

Command communication comes when there is a black and white, non-negotiable level of expectation, that the leader will not let something fall below that expectation.

Amy: It's the times where you have to break out "read my lips." Overused, it can be a dictatorship, but there are definitely, definitely times where urgency is at Its highest, and the leader has to draw the line in the sand.

Wayne: Exactly, and so that is a really important distinction to know you are engaged in a command decision or command communication. <u>Consultative</u> is two-way. It means that you are reaching a decision based on inquiry, and I think that's really important to think about. So much has been written about appreciative inquiry, and I invite the readers and listeners of this to explore appreciate inquiry further in terms of communication style.

The idea of consultative communication is really that you've asked a question, requested input, but you will be making the decision ultimately. It's important for your team to know at the outset that you are going to be making the decision because otherwise that becomes a miscommunication when they think that they're informing you and that you're going to do what they say.

Amy: Absolutely. Everybody remembers that horrible teacher who had the answer to the question, and just keeps asking the class until the class finally goes, "Look, if you know it, just say it."

Wayne: Right.

Amy: Why ask me in the first place?

Wayne: Making everybody wrong in the process.

And then the third one is <u>consensus</u>. This has to do with decision making. It also has to do with the way you are allowing a little more flow in your communication style. While a certain outcome is expected, you don't have to be involved in the actual decision making. You might ask the team members what they think. It's about getting a group discussion based on what the group itself wants, and from there, a decision is made by the group. You, as the leader, cannot come back in and tell them they are wrong or that you are doing it a different way. That would be back to the consultative-decision-making style.

One of the stories I tell actually comes from within Pride Institute, about coffee. Amy, at one point you, the CEO, got fed up with the team wanting approval at every step for what kind of coffee, how much coffee, who will get the coffee, when it will be procured, etc. As the CEO, you'd basically had enough of those piddly decisions coming your way, and you got very clear with the message: "I don't need to be in on this. You guys decide. The end result is coffee, right? I don't care what style, I don't care what flavor. The outcome I want is that there's coffee." I think what's really important in terms of communication is that the end result needs to be communicated, and when it really is not an urgent, life shattering, life changing decision to be made, leaving team members to make decisions, because that empowers them. And so that's part of the communication process as well.

Now that you know that there are three communication remedies, lets chat about how you ensure all three have the right impact. This happens when you embrace concepts of Meta Communication. The definition of Meta Communication Is communicating "beyond or outside of," and it shows up in a few different ways. Studies by Albert Mehrabian out of UCLA a few decades ago looked at how the meanings of messages were perceived. The question of "likability" was called into play, as well. The results were surprising and underscore the need for really looking at all aspects of communication.

The core concept of meta communication begins with the idea that words account for only about 7% of the meaning of any message. For example, if somebody hits your car and you said the words "thank you," they would sound very different than if someone told you won the lottery: "Thank you!!!" If you were mad at someone, your tone would sound different when you said "good morning" than your tone would be if you just saw the person that you were in madly in love with: "Goooood morrrrrning." That means that the words you say NEED 93% augmentation to convey a message's true meaning.

Tonality accounts for 38% of the meaning of a message. Tonality is pace, pitch, tone, and volume. If someone is speaking very fast or has what's called 'pressured' speech, there may be a reason for that. It may be that they are, in fact, under some pressure or feeling stressed. Or it could be that they are simply what's known as a "driver."

If someone speaks slowly, it could be that they're ponderous. Or it could also be that they are depressed. You have to take into account the other attributes along with pace, such as pitch. Is their pitch getting higher or lower? Remember that excitement shows up as high pitch, and depression shows up as lower pitch.

Command also shows up as lower pitch. So as a leader, you need to be congruent. This goes back to miscommunication. You could possibly be giving

Practice Verbal Skills

off the opposite Indicators than what you are actually saying when you are trying to communicate something.

Early on, about a few decades ago, I ran a psychiatric hospital, and the assistant director of nursing came to me after one of my team meetings and told me that I had a smile on my face during a time when I was saying that our budget was being cut and we were going to have to face layoffs. My communication was completely incongruent, and I realized that my intent was to make my message seem as if the bad news really wasn't so bad. Unfortunately, in this instance, being more congruent would have been much, much, much more effective by showing concern versus showing happiness.

So, look at what you're saying and how you're saying it. Pace, pitch, tone —it's easy to go from concern to condescension in an instant—make sure that your tone matches your intent. Pace, pitch, tone… and…

Rapport

Volume is next in this list, and that is how loud are you speaking. I have just recently met with somebody who's got a great big booming voice, and that's his style of how he shows happiness. The problem is that's also how he shows concern. That's how he shows anger. That's how he shows pretty much everything, and so his great big booming voice doesn't vary.

So volume is a big deal.

Amy: That's good. It reminds me of one of the very first pieces of feedback you ever gave me. I'll never forget it. I could never understand why people would say to me that as a leader I wasn't open to ideas. When we finally had the feedback chat, the following realization came to both of us. Bottom line: in normal day to day activities, I am a happy, peppy girl! When I get engaged in a new concept or very interested in what somebody is sharing with me, I smile less, my eyebrows knit together like I'm wearing an extra sweater, and unfortunately It can look unbelievably judgmental, which is the exact opposite of how I'm truly feeling!

Wayne: Exactly! And I was so relieved when you got that eyebrows up is a more open facial expression than the closed one you were showing. You were being thoughtful when it looked like you were being judgmental.

Amy: It was such a "V8" moment for me, and once I shared this with the team, we became much more open and collaborative because everyone was on the same page when it came to perceived signals. That is a classic example of "meta communication is everything."

Wayne: It goes to the third piece of meta-communication. We have words accounting for 7%, tone accounting for 38%, and body language and facial expression accounting for 55% of the communication. So when you knit your brow and pursed your lips, to your mind that was interest. To the person who was speaking, it looked like disdain. And it ended up shutting down some vital communication. So, I'm glad you got that leadership lesson.

The truth is that while we communicate, over half of what we communicate comes through as body language and that body language is believed 100% of the time. That is evident when the waiter comes over and says, "You must try today's soup" but he's shaking his head no. "You must really try today's soup." (No... no, don't do it... nooooooo.)

So imagine you're doing a case presentation, and you are shaking your head no. In the back of your head what causes that no shaking is either that you don't believe what you're saying, or you are being concerned. Either way, it's coming out as incongruence.

Amy:

FINAL NUCKIN' FUTZ NUGGET OF THE CHAPTER:
This is why leadership is perception. It has absolutely nothing to do with what you said. It's how it's perceived.

When it comes to upping your impact as a leader, the first step has got to be your willingness to be accountable in communicating in an effective fashion. Don't over-communicate, don't under-communicate, and don't miscommunicate, because you won't get the response that you desire from your team. This is a key lesson we both have learned from the road.

CHAPTER 3

Leadership Styles - You Say Tomato...

oc but I will Do it my way

Amy: We now understand why we need a why. We have a better understanding of how to communicate the why, so that it's not empty air that people can respond too. I think the next real big lesson that we need to talk about is understanding and adapting your leadership styles.

- Who are you as a leader?

- How are you perceived?

- What's your persona? And is that persona likable? Believable?

- And... can you be flexible with your styles, based on the situation and individual needs?

Wayne: Right.

Amy: When adapting your style, are you Credible? Honest? And most important, able to inspire others to want to do what you want them to do?

Wayne: And often intentions are so different than the actual way that a person shows up. Being forceful and direct isn't always true leadership.

Amy: **NUCKIN' FUTZ NUGGET:** Leadership is all about perception. The scariest thing of all is that leadership is perception. You can believe that you are a wise and benevolent person; but what your team actually sees is the angry dictator, and you've got to own it.

Wayne: Or condescending.

Amy: Right. And you have to own it.

Wayne: Mm-hmm.

Amy: It is important for a leader to wake up in the morning and be able to put on a style that's comfortable for them, so that it doesn't feel forced, because we all know that if the team even sniffs a hidden agenda, you will be marked as less than believable as a leader!

Wayne: Indeed.

Amy: Once the team perceives your lack of believability, they will filter everything you say or do from that point forward. So the first point is how am I going to lead? And am I comfortable? Then the secondary point is: how will that be perceived?

[handwritten margin notes: "Verbal Skills"; "Debbie - Too wordy"; "Prestella - Too loud"; "Kristina - my way"; "Debbie to do Just Say"; "To adopt my own"; "Janet - Not enough (they)"]

Wayne: Exactly.

Amy: And both need to be congruent.

Wayne: That was the key word I was going to bring up; the word is congruent. It is just so darn important. Right? Leaders need to show up as credible and flexible. Those are two key traits that every leader needs. Being in alignment with beliefs is the way to show up as congruent.

In the previous chapter I disclosed one of the mistakes I made as a new leader, smiling when I had to deliver some bad news about downsizing. It made me look like some evil kind of king, or something—as if I was taking joy in this. I think that my intent was to make it easier to listen to, however I think the way it came across was, I am the administrator, and I'm actually really happy that I'm going to have to cut people's jobs.

Amy: Absolutely.

Wayne: That felt pretty horrible.

Amy: I think it's a point of maturity to be able to be comfortable enough in your own rightness and your own intentions, to be open to the fact that how your message is perceived is what moves the needle. In my early days as a leader, somebody would come into my office, and say, you know, I felt like you weren't listening to me. And my genuine stimulus/response was to want to pull out a scorecard, and show all the times I've ever cared, listened, and loved people and prove that person wrong. It was a point of pride that I needed to prove that my intentions were absolutely always correct.

Wayne: *"But I am a good listener. I do care about you."*

Amy: *"And remember that time three years ago, when I patted you on the back, and said nice job."* At a certain point you need to be confident enough as a leader that you can reconcile what you've done in the past and the current situation where this person doesn't feel cared for, listened to. Bottom line, you have to own it.

Wayne: And that's so important, right?

NUCKIN' FUTZ NUGGET: Credibility. Flexibility. Congruence. That's not a one-and-done kind of thing. That is every moment. The whole idea about congruence is, are you living into your best self? Are you modeling the way? And it really is about you first, dear leader. We're talking about leadership styles. So many of our leaders say it would be great to run this practice, or this business, if only my team would shape

up. And I liken that to somebody standing in front of a fireplace and saying, "I will give you wood when you give me warmth." It must be you first. You feed it. It's your job to feed into it, so that you get the response that you want back.

Amy: Absolutely, true … And congruence, and credibility going back to the earlier point, is that it ultimately has to be a style you are comfortable inhabiting. The old concept of "fake it till you make it" really doesn't work, because it's very hard to be congruent wearing some other leadership style clothes that don't fit you!

Wayne: Right.

Amy: Many women leaders fall into the leadership style trap of, "for me to compete as a woman leader I need to take on the mantle of being militaristic in my approach."

Wayne: Yes. I think it's just so important that people show up as congruent and credible. Be a good human; just start there.

Amy: Right.

Wayne: Yeah.

Amy: And you know the personality styles of the dentists that we serve aren't necessarily conducive to what you would see on a silver screen of the stereotypical traits of a leader, right? People tend to think of the leader being the bombastic, P.T. Barnum, rainmaker. The leader who knows all the answers. Is emphatic in approach. Doesn't suffer fools. And over communicates in a way that inspires, right? And that's not necessarily going to line up to the personality styles in the profession that we serve.

Wayne: I think that's really, really important. That you have a style, and it is not a stereotypical style. Your style is *your* style. And that's what people need from you as a leader. Here's the thing, do leadership styles change? Absolutely, and that's the point of this chapter as well. It's that you can demonstrate that you are moving, and changing, and evolving as a leader right in front of your team. And that can be any industry. It's dentistry. It's engineering. It could be anything, and it could be in front of your family too. I think sometimes what happens is that people feel like, well, I'm not getting the feedback that I'm changing. People can't see me change. It's gonna be slow, and gradual. Allow that to happen. The whole thing is you've got to push yourself to want to listen differently. To want to communicate differently. To put your vision out there differently. Right? Ultimately all those can come together.

Amy: That's a great point. Because going back to the need for congruence and credibility, you can learn and grow in your different leadership styles. You can learn to become more directive. You can learn to become more supportive. It requires practice.

Wayne: Yes.

Amy: It requires reinforcement. It requires the grace to know when you're wrong, and not doing that, and the pat on the back when you do. The jury is in on this one. Anyone can become an effective leader and exhibit the style that their followers need, if they actually roll up their sleeves, and do the hard work.

Wayne: Exactly. You have to start with your vision. It goes back to the earlier chapters where we focused on vision, and communication. What is it that you want to communicate? Who *are* you? What is your vision? What are your values? How are you letting those things be known? Those have to come through, primarily through your actions. And then if you're finding that you're not congruent, you've got to find a way to align. The whole idea of credibility is based in, *"say what you mean, and do what you say."* That's the credible piece. If you've got a project you're working on, or an outcome in mind, then say you've got this outcome in mind. Awesome. You communicate that to your team. Fantastic. Your team says, no I don't want to do it. And then you go okay, what's another idea? That's a problem. Instead, you say, "Uh, no.

Help people, give, support
like To help
people Iuprove

This is where we're headed, and team you're going to be on the path to doing this. Let's get this done." That's you being credible.

Amy: Yeah, and to take that one step farther. The good old standby *"you gotta walk your talk"* means that you not only have to stand by what it is that you believe, and say, and do. You have to do it. There's nothing worse than a leader calling his or her team into the icy waters of change, while he or she stands on the nice warm shore wrapped in a fluffy towel saying, "jump in and then tell me how it was."

Wayne: Right. Nothing worse. It comes back to modeling the way. As a leader, you have to show others what your expectations are. So again, it's you first, dear leader. You first.

Amy: Absolutely.

 **NUCKIN' FUTZ NUGGET:** To take this one step further, your team will not trust you, or trust your leadership, if you're not willing to get your hands dirty. If you're not willing to push the envelope. If you're not willing to go through the pain and itch of evolving right along with your team.

Wayne: In terms of communication, it is okay for your team to know that you are a little bit afraid of the change, or that you're uncertain. The part of leadership style we talked about is credibility, the other part is your flexibility. That means, the way you get there may not be the original way you have in mind, but the fact that you're committed to ultimately getting there, that's the credibility. The flexibility is that there may be different avenues to the desired outcome.

Amy: Well, that brings it right back to one of my made-up words. I'm famous for made up words.

Wayne: Yes. Yes Amy, you are!

Amy: I consider the number one leadership trait to be "unkillability." And "unkillability" means, as Scarlett O'Hara of Gone with the Wind said, "As God as my witness," we're going there, no matter what the obstacle or barrier. When you say there's a point B that you're driving your team toward, if you truly believe that you're going to get them there no matter what, then you're going to be much more flexible on the roadmap—the how to get to the Point B. You can stop at Q. You can stop at R. You can stop at T. Ultimately, if the team wants to take a little bit of a scenic tour, and head off the main road, an unkillable leader can say, ok team, take that tour, and remember we are going to wind up at Point B, no matter what! A leader who believes in their unkillability will always be willing to be flexible, and not micromanage the process. Be inflexible on the ultimate why, and goal, and vision. Be completely flexible with the road map to get there.

Wayne: Well, I think a great analogy is an airplane flight. An airplane takes off on a small strip of land on one side of the continent, flies thousands of miles, and lands on a really small strip of land on the other side of the continent, or around the world. And that plane is actually off course—it's off course ninety-seven percent of the time. What does that mean? That they've decided to change the outcome? No, they're headed for their very specific spot where they will land. They are using the instruments they have, and they are getting feedback along the way. They're making use of that feedback they get so they can ultimately land at the outcome they had in mind. On time. On budget. That is credibility, with a little bit of flexibility.

NUCKIN' FUTZ NUGGET: Make use of the feedback along the way while keeping the specific end result in mind!

Amy: Dr. Pride used to say, "Don't land in the corn fields. Land on the runway."

We have some amazing lessons from the road. The next that comes to mind is, learning talking the talk and walking the walk! There's nothing worse than that leader who thinks they have to be the Wizard of Oz as their dominant style. Imagine, the wizard behind the curtain, the great and powerful Oz, that spews fire, power, and crushes anyone who questions along the way. The wizard has to always be right in order to maintain the myth of greatness and power. Just remember what ultimately happened to the wizard. Eventually, Toto snuck behind the curtain, and found out the wizard was mortal and fearful. And that happens with our doctors all the time. Because if you are projecting yourself as the great and powerful Oz, someone on your team will sneak behind your curtain and find your vulnerability. And they will exploit it, right?

Wayne: Right.

Amy: I have a great story. I had a female doctor who chose not to be the stereotypical sorority sister. She went more toward the mini-Hitlerette side of life.

Wayne: Uh-oh.

Amy: She felt because she was in this position of being a female that it was her word, her ways. Always, always, always. Her team was on a reward shopping spree, and they were supposed to have an hour and a half to spend whatever money she had given out. And they had to spend it on something that they really wanted. Well, I actually got a phone call from a team member, sobbing while at the store, which was unusual. I asked "what's going on?" And she said, "I bought a pool cover." My response was, "Well, that doesn't really make sense to me, but if you wanted it..." Her response was, "But no, you don't understand—I don't own a pool!" Now, that wasn't the sad part. When "Dr. Dictator" heard what she had done, her response was, "Sorry, it's the rules, your time's up, you have to keep the pool cover." Now, what was the purpose of the team building? Reward and recognition of a team that performed above and beyond, right? As I coached the doctor through her self-righteousness, with clenched teeth I emphatically suggested that she let her team member take back the pool cover. Dr. Dictator's concern was, if I break the rules, nobody is going to believe that I'm a strong leader, and they'll bend the rules for everything. In this situation, the team will not learn the lesson of strong leadership, they will learn that the doctor is not a very nice or empathetic human! Don't forget—the strongest leaders know when to be flexible.

Wayne: Exactly. And it has to do with what was communicated up front. Understanding the intent. Again, it's what is the intention in doing a team building exercise like that? What's the intention of pulling your team together?

Let's talk about another leadership style we have seen on the road. You are sort of the queen of neologisms, the made-up words, and there are some other words that you use for leaders, which are kind of funny. The one leader where we... Well... We've all seen the leaders who bury their heads in the sand. They've been called ostrich leaders before, and we have a different term, and it's for the kind of person who goes, well, maybe if I ignore it, the problem will go away. Maybe if I ignore it, the problem will just resolve by itself. And we all know that those problems never resolve by themselves. In fact, they always complicate. And Amy, your term for that kind of leader is...?

Amy: Dr. Weenie! And the running joke is you may be a Dr. Weenie if you have a team member who has a conflict and you take a vacation and hope that individual goes into a coma before you ever have to talk to him or her. Add an E to the word for every year you have failed to nip conflicts in the bud, which makes some doctors weenies on steroids.

Wayne: Indeed.

Amy: They are the Barry Bonds of weenies. This is the classic:

"Is there a staff member that doesn't line up to your vision?"

"Yes, absolutely, I hate seeing her. She hates seeing me. She does nothing to promote the vision, and values."

And the next question is, "how long has she been working and bothering you?"

And the answer is, "Oh, twenty-five plus years."

Wayne: Exactly. I have a very specific example of somebody that came through our program. He talked to us in one of our first sessions about hearing one of his front desk team members cussing in front of patients. And I had a reaction to hearing that. Using pull communication and trying to get the doctor to take ownership, I inquired and guided the conversation, "Well this probably needs to be rectified. Don't you think doctor?"

He said something like, "well, yes. She was also found kissing one of the patients in the hallway."

Imagine us having this conversation now. I'm fully perplexed. "Doctor, the same person that was cussing is also kissing patients. Is that appropriate?"

The doc got a little sheepish and admitted, "Well, no. I should probably do something about it."

I'm thinking, he should probably do something about it. But, I'm now intrigued as to why it's gone on so long. "Well, that's true, Doctor. What is it about her? Why have you kept her?"

He replied, "Well, she's vital at the front desk."

I'm certain that pretty much everyone is replaceable. "Well, that's good, and I'm thinking you could probably find somebody else."

And then he blurts out, "Yes, and she's been stealing from me. I'm pretty sure she's been embezzling."

Wait, whatttt? I shook my head, "She's cussing in front of your clientele. She's kissing your clientele in the hallway, and you think she's been stealing. How long has this been going on?"

"Eighteen years."

"What? Whatttttt?"

These stories are real stories for you, dear reader, to recognize that you may not be alone. That you may have been ignoring some things that you know deep down need to be taken care of.

 **NUCKIN' FUTZ NUGGET:** This is a matter of courage. Right? We've talked about clarity. We've talked about how you're showing up in your congruence with your energy. This is about courage, and really what are the things that you are stepping into? Or —and more important, I guess— what are the

things that you're stepping away from when you really think, or know deep down, that you need to be stepping *in*?

Amy: Absolutely. And the very sad part to all of that, is that your team will absolutely judge you by the way you handle the weakest link.

Wayne: Too true.

Amy: And so, if you're going to have—or hope for—a culture of personal growth, fulfillment, intention, and significant impact, then you need to be the right kind of leader. If you are not confronting the poor performer, you ain't never gonna get the superstar. And that's absolutely the problem we almost always deal with in our leadership coaching. The continued point about the Dr. Weenie and the poor performer, is that in lieu of confronting the behavior or lack or result, the Dr. Weenie takes the monkey on their own back, or they overburden the superstar.

Wayne: Right.

Amy: So being a weenie has many more ramifications than strictly having a staff member that's not living up to your vision, and values, and strategies. It is _the_ rotten apple that will ruin the basket.

Wayne: That is so very true. Yeah, so you've got to ask yourself whether you are taking it on because you're afraid of guiding a team member. Or, perhaps you are punishing the great performer by giving that performer more, and more, and more to do because you're afraid of actually being the leader, the manager, or both.

Be in the leadership role the way that your team, your family, and your community need you to be.

Amy: You know, Wayne, as you think about the characteristics that support the different styles, one of the things that's very important for any leader to understand, is that no matter what your style is, it needs to move toward either you are supplying or delivering direction to your team or supplying or delivering support. It's almost like a Meritage wine, a beautiful mixture.

NUCKIN'FUTZ NUGGET: The wisest leader knows how much direction is needed, how much support is needed, and when you blend them correctly you get motion in your ocean.

Wayne: The trick to that, Amy, is that it's a moving target. Just when you think that everybody gets this much support, and everybody gets this much direction, that you realize that it's not an everybody thing. The seasoned leader finds that each glass of that Meritage needs a little bit different amount of direction or different amount of support, and that changes over time too.

Amy: Well it changes situationally as we all know. There's the chronic basic level of support and direction each individual comes needing—nine times out of ten they default to this level of need. And then there is the very important curiosity factor of what am I seeing in this situation and what blend of our direction support wine is needed.

Wayne: Exactly, so for example, in a dental practice that's implementing cad-cam based treatment or any kind of new technology that requires a certain amount of learning, the doctor has to be ready to guide. That is, give direction as well as encourage. And then to take a deep breath and to expect that it's not going to be perfect the first time.

Amy: Right, and again on a matrix, the more you change your blend, the better off the results are going to be. So it takes a heavy dose of diagnosis to be able to give that individual talent or team member what it is that he or she needs.

Wayne: In the moment. In the moment, right.

Amy: Part of what I see that goes very, very wrong in many offices is because dentists tend to be perfectionists, and I don't think that that's just exclusive to dentists -

Wayne: That's true.

Amy: That pretty much goes to many a leader. When you hear the concern that we see on confidential questionnaires of the team feeling over-managed, micro-managed, anally managed, that's an example to me of way too much direction and not enough support. Because support to me does not just mean, hey I'm here for you. Support means I'm giving you the resources you need, I'm giving you the space you need, I'm giving you the acknowledgment and connection that you need, and it's two-way versus one-way which is very hard for someone who is white-knuckling themselves on that team member's goal, task or skill that's very hard to actually pull off. So it seems on paper, that support would be easier. I actually see that support is harder because, to quote Frozen, you have to, "let it go."

Wayne: You know what's interesting is that in many ways this is like parenting—That you can't treat every child the same, that a toddler needs something different than a six-year-old, and that six-year-old needs something different than a 12 year old, and that great direction is needed maybe with different language at each different developmental stage. That boundaries are always needed. You talked about giving space. That is huge, because the person who is doing the thing and trying it out for the first time, or doing it again for the 12th time, or showing that they can do it all by themselves—they need space, and they need a good leader to step in and say, "I am here." It's either I'm here waiting for you at the finish line, or I'm here running side by side with you, or I'm here cheering you on from the sidelines...

Amy: Or take my hand, I'll take you.

Wayne: Yes, and that's the direction-and-support beautiful blend that is the Meritage.

Amy: Absolutely, we all know that when you assume less direction and support is needed, it makes a donkey of you and me; we're not using the biblical word (whispering: Ass) right now. The fact of the matter is that Doctor Pride used to say when you find yourself on a dead horse, get off. If you're directing, and no growth is happening, try supporting! If it's not having a perceived result in competence, in mastery, in confidence, in inspiration, then change the blend of your wine.

Wayne: **NUCKIN FUTZ NUGGET: I think a key word there, Amy, is if it's not having the *perceived* change or *perceived* movement that you want, *your* perception counts as the leader.**

Your perception counts. So, too, does the perception of the person who's doing it, because they may see it as huge growth. Another example would be learning a new language or learning to play a musical instrument. For somebody who is a master and says 'just play the flipping song,' that's different than somebody who's learning their first notes on a piano, finding middle C, or finding their first chords. So as a leader, we are responsible for saying "This is what the terrain is, this is what this musical instrument is capable of, this is where I want you to focus, try it this way, let me see you try it."

Amy: Exactly, and another style of direction and support that can go horribly wrong is the concept of command versus collaborate.

Wayne: That is so right Amy! You are on a roll here!

Amy: Command is that militaristic, General Patton-like do this or I'll kill you. The doctor drive-by or the leader drive-by. Collaboration, when it's approached the wrong way or over-collaborated, can be like the fraternity brother or sorority sister where 'let's link hands and everybody has to agree' or no motion in the ocean ever occurs. A dynamic of that is there are times to command— when the building's on fire you don't sit down and say, "how does everybody feel about making it toward the emergency exit?" And yet there's also if it's not on fire, eventually you do have to say, "and how do you feel about this, and what would you do differently, and am I okay to actually find that the sum of the whole is greater than its parts."

Wayne: The important point here, I think, is exactly that. That there are times to command. The problem is that command can be disguised as collaboration. When I was consulting with a major national company, one of the division heads was... well, he surprised me with his statement because I was looking for collaboration. I was looking to see how he would collaborate with these other divisions, and he said, "I collaborate just fine. If they would just do it my way, the collaboration would go absolutely smoothly."

What's funny about that is that he was absolutely serious, that he didn't see the irony in his "do it my way and we'll be collaborating just fine," command. He saw it as collaboration, and that is something that is a trap for leaders.

Amy: A couple of years ago, we had a feeling that the staff meetings that our dentists were facilitating were more command versus collaboration, so I had several guinea pig doctors actually video their staff meetings—just to have the camera on naturally so that they got used to it. One of my favorite examples was a doctor who insisted that he never ever actually interceded, that everything was generated by his team, and orally he said very little. But what I found so amusing when I actually observed the tape is every time a question came up, before it would get answered or a decision was made, eyes would immediately go to the CAPO, the commander in chief. If the commander in chief did not smile or shake his head then it did not happen. So though no words were spoken, it was absolutely a militaristic jamboree, so to speak, because he was holding that meeting in check, just like your example did.

Wayne: Yes. The non-verbal cues are huge, and this goes both ways too. We talked about the doctor drive-by or the one that's fully in command. The opposite is true with the person who dares not speak up because he or she fears the judgment of his team members or her team members. So the affectionate term that we impose on the opposite of the "drive-by," is the "doctor weenie," and rather than make a command decision, that kind of leader often makes no decision.

Amy: Which isn't collaboration either.

Wayne: No, it's neither command nor collaborative. In fact, it only serves to disappoint and make all the team members irate.

Amy: Absolutely. So you know one of the things that I always hear from the leaders that I coach and consult is there are a lot of parts and pieces, and how do you wake up and go, *"am I supposed to be applying direction or support, am I commanding versus collaborating, what's my style, am I doing this "leadership stuff"* *right?"* For me, the synthesis of this is that there are two distinct roles that every team member deserves to have access to in their leadership and those roles I call coach versus counselor. The analogy I like to use is that coaching is the Miracle Grow. It's to take the little seedlings of knowledge, skills, abilities, and attitudes in your garden and to pour all the nutrition on it, and through it, and around it, so that it grows into even stronger knowledge, skills and abilities.

Counseling is the Weed Be Gone. It's to correct inappropriate behavior, decisions, or outcomes, with consequence. When you're thinking about direction and support and all those other things, then that combo of direction and support when you're coaching is going to look very different from direction and support if you're counseling. The dance steps that I'd like to invite every leader to get comfortable with are:

- When should I be coaching? (Which means I'm pulling the best skills and results out of my team)

- When should I be counseling? (Which means I'm pulling the weeds out of my practice "garden", by correcting inappropriate behaviors with levels of consequence)

Wayne: Again you've got some key points in there. One of them is the word *deserve*.

NUCKIN' FUTZ NUGGET: Every team member deserves to have coaching and counseling where appropriate. They deserve it, and as a leader it's your duty/obligation to actually provide that. The difference in coaching versus counseling does tie back to direction and support. I like to use a sports analogy even though I'm not much of a sports guy and that's where if you were coaching golf or basketball or baseball you'd be focused on a person's use of their wrist, how are they moving that object to be able to hit their target. Whatever that target is, goes for bowling, whatever it is. The wrist, the hips, the shoulder's alignment, all of that ties together. Now as somebody who is doing direction and counseling you're going to say very specifically "move your right wrist one quarter inch here, this way, step in this much, shift your weight that much, breathe out here." That's direction setting and very clearly counseling.

Coaching is more of "hey, you missed your shot by four inches, up to the right can you correct that?" It allows the person to step in and actually correct it on his or her own because they have the ability to see it, and they have the desire to hit that target

Amy: It's funny because I actually look at counseling a little bit differently. I would consider your first example still coaching but in the learning/doing band. When a coach is first coaching it's more directive because I am saying hold your wrist this way. It becomes more supportive when it's I've seen you do it now show me. Because now we're just reinforcing the do as we look at this. Counseling, to me, would be when after numerous attempts to coach your team member, they're still not getting it and it's essential to the overall strategy of the business itself or it violates the vision. The role of counselor would be you have been coached, there is now a potential negative consequence, and the negative consequence isn't necessarily drop kick through the goal post and flag. The negative consequence could be a job shift, it could be lack of a reward, or lack of a wage increase, or probation, or depending on the level of severity you can no longer work here. The counseling band to me is when you can no longer tolerate the weeds in your garden.

Wayne: It makes a lot of sense, Amy, to re categorize it as two levels of coaching. One is much more hands on and in the startup of learning a new skill; the other is much more hands off and perhaps more leadership than management in that case. Then the idea of counseling, being, you've been given the opportunity to swing the bat, you've been given the opportunity to make the shot, you've been given the opportunity to set the tray in the operatory a very specific way or do the sterilization a very specific way, and the way you're doing it is not good enough.

I have an example from one of my doctors who requires that all of his team members, if they're doing sterilization, wear gloves. One of the team members couldn't see the reason for doing that. This was a command versus collaborative decision. This was his desire to see better safety and better environmental protection for the sake of the employee, and she refused time after time. She was coached, she was shown where to get gloves, she was talked to about when to use gloves, and it's so simple. It's a simple task. You would think, do this at this point. You walk into the sterilization room—it's the time to put gloves on. She couldn't get it, and that's where counseling kicked in. Unfortunately for her, that's when the decision was made after several attempts to counsel, that weed was pulled from that garden.

Amy: The truth of the matter is that the doctor weenies of the world are so afraid of counseling that they fail to coach, and I do believe in my heart of hearts that the 80/20 rule applies here: 80% coaching and 20% counselling. The good news is, if you don't like counseling or if you're afraid because of your style of counseling, coach more. The idle hands are the devil's workshop. If there is coaching occurring and you are giving your team member, your talent, every opportunity to be successful, when you do have to counsel it's black and white. You can wake up in the middle of the night and say he or she has been coached to the very depths of their soul, and it's still not happening. Something has to change, I need to counsel—there's a weed in the garden.

Wayne: And that's by having very clear targets. Performance targets. Do this, this way; make this goal this many times. Whether that's a collections goal, whether that's a conversion, whether that's a smile every time you answer the phone goal, it's very clear. It's very measurable, and that's where coaching can happen. And certainly, that's where you can step in and offer counseling.

Amy: And the collaboration part is that it's mutually agreed upon mastery and results. It takes two to mutually agree upon mastery and results; it takes one to say these results either measure to my vision, values or strategy, or they don't because I love living in the world of black and white. If you assume these styles, the right mix, the right role, then you will be able to lead your team in that world that doesn't have gray.

Wayne: I have two more points just bouncing off what you just said. The first is measurement.

NUCKIN' FUTZ NUGGET: If you can't measure it, then what are you counseling to? If you can't measure it, what are you coaching to? You've got to be able to say "this is the outcome, this specifically is the outcome." And the other thing besides measurement is to be able to offer that feedback, "did it happen or didn't it?" So, again, that puts you back in the either coach or counselor role, and you must talk about what you're seeing. Have a defined outcome, offer the coaching and support, offer the direction and support, offer the coaching to that place, and if they can't make it, it's time for counseling.

Amy: Absolutely, and honestly your team likes structure.

NUCKIN' FUTZ NUGGET: Your team will love black and white parameters as long as they are wide, and as long as, as you said, they are thoroughly communicated.

So, Wayne, at this point we've given our leaders the ability to deliver the why, communicate it in an effective way and in a style that actually keeps the motion going in your ocean, and these are the basic lessons that separate the superstar from the mediocre. So we are keep on keeping on.

Wayne: Yep, and what we're left with now is **A NUCKIN' FUTZ NUGGET:** *as a leader you choose your style and, like any art, it is crafted a day at a time. Keep honing.*

Amy: Stay curious my friends.

CHAPTER 4

Creating Inspired Followers - Where you Lead I will Follow!

No DRAWA Just RupSum

Amy: You know, Wayne, there's been book after book after book written about all of the talents and traits that go into great leaders. However, the leader can only be as great as the follower. There is an art and science to creating a culture that inspires excellent followership, and that kind of completes the circle as far as I'm concerned.

Wayne: It does. We want followers that do not just follow blindly like little sheep, but rather followers that end up supporting the Vision and ultimately the business.

Amy: **NUCKIN' FUTZ NUGGET:** When you say followers don't have to be sheep—followers can be dynamic, they can be worker bees. They can be invested team leaders, however the follower chooses to follow. Which means it's up to the leader to create an environment where that whole spectrum makes that choice to be a follower. I don't know about you...

well, you and I have both experienced being leaders in our own right.

Wayne: Yes!

Amy: And also, willing followers. There are certain things that we look for in an environment that makes us willing and able to follow something or someone that we truly believe in.

Wayne: Right, so it's up to each leader to create an environment that allows for the best of each individual to show up, and sometimes individual employees can only give so much. They don't have the capacity either energetically or intellectually, or maybe in some other way, to show up. But that said, I think it's up to the leader to create an environment that invites each employee to show up at their best.

Amy: You know, that's right, and of course, the first person that I think about is Dr. Pride. Our legacy leader here at the Pride Institute. One of the things that I'll never forget is after I went through 11 years being an independent consultant and I was going through the very difficult interview process to actually get hired. By the time I actually sat down with Dr. Pride, it was kind of the pinnacle, and I was ready. He shoved the philosophy statement in my face and had me read the section that referred to the team, and it started with Pride Institute's greatest asset. Paraphrased, it's people that are excited about being part of Pride, who are the best in what they do, who are motivated to achieve results, who always go above and beyond. And after I read it he took his great big bear paw and he placed his hand on that section and he said, 'There's a rumor going around that you're one of these.' And my response was, 'Put me in coach.' And that's an example of a culture connection that made a very independent leader choose to be a follower.

Wayne: You bet. You bet! Showing up at your best—it's where your personal vision matches the company vision. If you didn't have a personal desire to *be* your best, if you didn't have a personal desire to *show up at your best*, then any vision would do. Here, the Vision made so much sense. I had the good fortune of working both with and internally at AAA, working both with and internally at Whole Foods Market, and now here at Pride Institute. Really, each of those companies have visions that resonated with my own personal sense of who I am. Here at Pride Institute, it was complete, total alignment, where the match was incredible, and I think that's really what we want to create for any employee. That's why starting with vision makes so much sense. This, being the Followers section, really does bring that concept full circle. Starting with vision is so important. What is it that you, dear leader, believe in? And who are you choosing to gather around you?

Amy: You know, what I call one of the most controversial lines in the vision statement that I created for the Pride

Institute is that, "we attract good people who want to better themselves and others." That statement, to me, meant two things: it meant the internal customer, our team; and our external customer, the clients, that we choose to serve the finest information and counsel. That actually had a bit of a controversy because, of course, at Pride, we wanted to be great. This gave me a chance to set a culture for both leadership and followership because to me, not all great people are good, but all good people can be great, and a fundamentally good person to me, means I trust you. I respect you, I honor you because you have value, and trust, and respect others. That's one of the things that I think is really important, is that followers will follow when there are clear black and white, wide swimming lanes.

Wayne: Exactly, I'm going to encourage our readers to look back at the top of that last paragraph one more time. I want to impress on you, dear reader, that it's really about gathering good people. What is the "goodness" fit of the people you gather around you? That's totally, completely up to you!

Amy: Absolutely.

Wayne: **NUCKIN' FUTZ NUGGET: Also, creating true followers means that you are being clear about your expectations.** Being able to delegate appropriately means having clear expectations about what a very positive outcome might be.

Amy: Well, it's really interesting because I know that some of the deadest carcasses that we have encountered on the road are the dead initiatives of, *"I thought this was delegated, and it wasn't."* And what that means, is:

- It wasn't done at all

- Or, it wasn't done to the level of quality I expected

- Or, it wasn't done with any kind of purpose in mind

- Or it was actually done, but resulted in a negative effect.

So creating excellent followers who recognize their swim lanes is an art and science of delegation to its highest purpose and form.

Wayne: And when it's not done, or not followed up on, or any of those things, it means that the leader *thought* it was done and basically gave it away. And by giving it away, that's not delegation, that's abdication. That's stepping down from the leadership role and just giving it all away with fingers crossed that what you hoped might get done actually will.

Become Investor

Amy: Right, because abdication means "I no longer have any personal investment in success." If we go back to the leadership style of direction and support, effective delegation is little or no direction and little or no support, but never none, all the time. There has to be some kind of a feedback loop so that the person who is empowered and emancipated to do what it is that you want them to do feels the context and the breadth and the understanding that there is still a leader watching their back. I think that's an essential element of delegation.

Wayne: Agreed.

Amy: **NUCKIN' FUTZ NUGGET: One of the things that is a common mistake, is that delegation cannot occur until there is mutually agreed upon, demonstrated, consistent mastery of the job, the task, or the skill.** What I mean by that is that it's not, "Alright, I want you to handle all of the systems and protocols that it takes to schedule. Any questions? No? Good."

Wayne: No. That's really not good at all.

Amy: "I'm done, right?" The fact of the matter is, if we're talking about keeping the coffee maker stocked in the reception area that mutually agreed upon demonstrated mastery can be 10 seconds or less. When it's an entire system, it can be a very lengthy process depending upon the knowledge, skills, and ability of the person that you're attempting to delegate to.

Wayne: And I think what's important here is that you can have what's called successive approximations, and that means that with each skill there are certain tasks that go along with that skill. So, you coach and counsel as appropriate to each small task that builds into each skill. You don't ask a whale to jump out of a tank to the 20-foot level. You ask a whale to jump out of a tank to the one-foot level and reward it. Then the four-foot level and reward it. And so on up to the 20-foot level. It's a step-by-step process to the outcome you're after.

Amy: Right! How do you eat an elephant? One bite at a time.

Wayne: Exactly! Or climb a mountain? A step at a time!

Amy: You know, it's not usual when we're talking about job description or job expectations to basically just throw up all of the expectations with the understanding of, 'because I said it, now you got it.' I think that one of the other points that I want to make, and keep saying, is that: mutually agreed upon demonstrated mastery. Just because a team member says they have it, doesn't mean that it has been demonstrated yet. So there is a responsibility, an accountability, for the leader who is delegating to be very clear that this gets delegated, when we both have seen, over a consistent period of time, an outcome that is worthy of mastery. Until that's done so that there isn't abdication, that leader has to be watching that person with supervision.

Spuel Training

Wayne: I think an example here would be asking an assistant to contour design some kind of cad-cam based crown, without seeing the assistant be able to use the equipment to design appropriately. You're not going to just let it go and say, *"Okay, this patient needs this thing, go do it. Have at it."*

Amy: The classic answer from the "Serious Potato Heads" that we coach is, *"well how long exactly?"* and my running response is, *"3 minutes, 22 seconds."* The fact of the matter is how long you wait and hold out for mastery is ridiculously situational. It goes from the coffee maker all the way to experiencing complete mastery of insurance coding and processing of insurance benefits. It's not only dependent on the size and the scope of the task, but the knowledge, skills, abilities and attitudes that the person starts with foundationally. So there has to be two-way communication, there has to be a set training plan, learning, doing.

Wayne: So in terms of KSA's, Amy, you were talking about the knowledge, skills, abilities and attitudes, and I think it's really important to focus back on abilities because sometimes, people have capacity, but they don't always show up with the skill level built in. Circling back to what we talked about previously in terms of guiding or supporting, directing or supporting: That's where you delegate to the level of the skill, and you build to the level of the ability, and hopefully as their skills build, so to do their abilities, their desire even to learn more, and to perform better.

Amy: You know, that's a great point because the statement, "Use your talent wisely" comes to mind.

NUCKIN' FUTZ NUGGET: Not everybody is supposed to be first-string, but first-string can't be effective, unless there's an equally, effective second-string right behind them, to be able to keep the game going, to keep the momentum going.

So that leads to the next point of not everybody on your team has to be superstars. The great Ken Blanchard always said, "If you treat everybody equally, you're treating most unequally," and this goes to whether we're talking about delegation or even placing your team in the right positions where they can excel the most. What you were just saying about skill and aptitude is that a big mistake you can make is to take an excellent, clinical assistant and because they're so good chairside and basically telepathically knowing what instrument you need before you know you need it, and then assuming that person's going to be a great clinical team leader is an example of "stinkin' thinking."

Wayne: It really is. Way back in the... Was it the 60s or the 70s? That dates me, but think about...

Amy: Groovy...

Wayne: Yes, back in the 60s it was "groovy, baby." So, yeah, it was way back about 50-plus years ago when the concept of the Peter Principle showed up. That's where someone is promoted to the level of their incompetence. You don't want to just push somebody and push somebody. "You're so good at this. Now we're going to promote you to this other place where you have no skill or ability or even desire."

With that, dear leader, look around your team. Think of your team right now—who on your team stands out as, "Wow! They can meet anybody." and who on your team stands out as somebody like, "They're so withdrawn." Different people have different personalities, and even the withdrawn types can get stuff done. They may not be you. Your definition of superstar, I think is... I think it needs to be better defined too. What makes a superstar on anybody's team?

Amy: Exactly. It reminds me of when you and I teach our First-Level Leadership workshop and we're talking about the fact that even though we're huge fans of the vision and philosophy statement, they will never act as a silver bullet, when it comes to inspiring team members. There are gradient levels of chronic commitment within the team that each leader is going to have to deal with, individually! By chronic commitment I mean that whether due to nature or nurture, each individual tends to wind up at the same level of commitment... for the most part! As you get to know your team, remember that situationally, anyone can have a "bad hair day" when it comes to their commitment and motivation. If it's chronic, that means, 9 times out of 10 they land in the same place. As you're waking up in the middle of the night, thinking about, *"I know exactly what are they going to say to me next!"* that's where you're picking up the chronic commitment level. If we go back to the concept of using your talent wisely, if you understand the chronic commitment level of each member of your team you will be able to give them what they need in order to support your goals and strategies.

In order for your practice to be able to move forward successfully, there are two levels of chronic commitment that cannot be in your business for your vision to succeed. Those are the chronically apathetic and the chronically non-compliant staff member. From that point forward, it's blue skies ahead. The next two levels are the grudgingly compliant and the formally compliant.

Wayne: So true. Amy. You don't want somebody who says, "I won't do what you say, and I don't care."

Amy: Exactly, because those types of people are dangerous, and they'll suck the energy out of your vision, your inspiring why, and anything and everything you have hoped for. However, the next step up is the grudgingly compliant and the formally compliant, and these are what we would label your worker bees.

Wayne: Sure.

Amy: One's a little less disgruntled. A grudgingly compliant worker bee can still fulfill your vision and your goals, and then some. The formally compliant worker bee is very happy just working. The biggest 'aha', dear leaders, is that worker bees need to be told precisely what to do, to feel safe and secure. They are going to need to be directed, as we learned, and supported, and won't necessarily be where you go to delegate team leadership and ownership. Use your worker bees wisely, right? Above and beyond that are the genuinely compliant and the enrolled. This is where delegation team leadership can happen—less direction, more support. This is where you're going to have people who walk side by side with you and be the very deepest, invested follower. And again, an office full of those can succeed and go anyplace or anyhow they want to go.

Wayne: I think one of the mistakes that leaders make is to want that so badly that they pull a grudgingly compliant team member aside and say, "You're going to be enrolled now. You're going to own this portion of the practice or you're going to own this section.

NUCKIN' FUTZ NUGGET: Delegating to someone who barely wants to show up to do their job is a really bad idea. All the internal conversations of, "*If only* she would do this, *if only* he would act this way"— they don't get to the point of actually changing the behavior or the style. The grudgingly compliant have a working style that needs guidance to build them into great followers.

Amy: Yeah, and by the way, "Dr. Weenies" out there—Be careful what you wish for, because we both know that the most difficult commitment level to lead is the enrolled employee, because that denotes that you have to be in front of them. An enrolled employee is as committed as you can possibly be without being the owner of the biz. What we have seen along the way is that damage is done when the enrolled employee is more committed than the leader/owner themselves. That truly can create 'bull in a china shop' issues, because eventually the enrolled individual is going to burn out. If you as the leader, feel like you are chronically a grudgingly compliant worker at heart, never recruit an enrolled team member! You need to want to achieve your vision and goals at least as much as your most motivated employee!

Wayne: YES! And that means, _you_ get better. As a leader, you have to push yourself to get better. "Use your talent wisely," could mean gathering people around you that force you to be a better leader. And if you think about it, that is kind of an awesome thing.

Now the flip side: what happens when you gather all these people together? All these people come together and you want to have this thing called a team meeting? So this team meeting happens, you've gathered people around, and now they stare at you.

Amy: Or they vomit and spew at you.

Wayne: Or they whine and tell you all the things wrong with the business, right?

Amy: Or the loudest in the room is chattering on about something, and the rest of the formally compliant folks are just hoping that they'll melt into insignificance at some point.

Wayne: Yes, meanwhile everyone is watching the clock, hoping that they could just get through another one, and check off that they've had a team meeting.

Amy: Right. Also known as 'death by meetings.'

Wayne: Yes.

Jω — put Forth the effort

Amy: Also known as meetings from hell.

Wayne: And the meetings of the zombies, right?

Amy: Yeah.

Wayne: So, you show up and you get the blank stares, or you get the vomit and spew, or you get the loud one, or all quiet. And ... that can go on for years, can't it!

Amy: Honestly, team meetings are the coach's opportunity to formally address the combined talents of their team. Not just a drive-by in the lab. Not just the once a year, formal, individual growth conference. The team meetings are the opportunity to set the plays and strategies for the day, the week, the month, the year, and make sure that you've got team consensus and collaboration, so that you can move forward. The goal is to make sure the team is moving with you, not against you. I think that a lot of leaders conduct and tolerate meetings because they know they are supposed to have meetings.

Wayne: Right, they're based in "supposed to." It's a checklist item, "I'm supposed to have a meeting; I have no idea what to do with it.."

NUCKIN' FUTZ NUGGET: Well the meeting is the place to talk about expectations. What are the expectations of the business performance? How has each division or department done in terms of performance? In the dental practice, what was the production? What were the collections? How is the hygiene department doing? How many new patients did you get? So you're really tracking and talking about statistics in a way that you follow up with tracking trends and talking about why they matter. It's looking at the "so what" of it all and making sure that what you're talking about actually matters to each team member.

Amy: Right.

Wayne: It's the WIIFM (what's in it for me) and the "so what" of it all. Again, what are the things that matter to each team member? They have things that they'd like to say but it's not a gripe session. It's not a place to just air complaints; a team meeting is a place to come with potential solutions, as well.

Amy: Well, the crybabies who mope take us all the way back to the first chapter. The meetings which are so important have to start with why. The "why" of the meeting reveals the "how" of the meeting and the "what" of the meeting. And that "why" of the meeting has got to be more inspiring than, *"We're supposed to get together once a month and have a moment of silence for all the things that we didn't do!"*

Celebrate

Wayne: Right.

Amy: As a key tool to inspire followers, a clearly defined why will rally the troops toward a common denominator so that they can then praise progress as they execute the action plan.

NUCKIN' FUTZ NUGGET: The other thing that I think is very important is to clarify the purpose and the expected outcomes of the meeting. Is this meeting that is for consensus—is this a meeting for the loudest voice wins? Is this a meeting for analysis? Is this a meeting for problem solving and execution of an action-plan? These expectations become very important to set before you jump into it with both feet.

Wayne: Exactly, so setting expectations about performance, setting expectations about outcomes—whether it's a meeting or an individual performance—that's going to be something that's foundational throughout all of this. So what are your expectations of every meeting? What're you hoping to have as an outcome? And as a leader, knowing what your desired outcome is, before you gather people together. You have to know ahead of time what you want them thinking about. This is influence, by the way, and you need to focus back on what you want them thinking about and what you want them to feel, and then take action on at the end of each meeting. And knowing that, what are you going to do as a leader to set the stage to have the correct discussions and to pull? This is a place for pull — you're providing thoughtful questions to pull responses from each of your team members.

Amy: Keeping in mind that those team members, aka followers, are grudgingly compliant, formally compliant, genuinely compliant and enrolled. And each one has a significant voice and a contribution to be made. So one of the challenges is always, how do we truly get consensus when people process differently, communicate differently, learn differently. And whether it's the good old how many of you agree put your thumb up, or on a scale of 1-10 how close, the leader has to be smart enough to be able to hear the quietest of voice, and sometimes quiet the loudest. Being one of the loudest, I can tell you that's a challenge unto itself.

Wayne: Quiet down, Amy!

Amy: Exactly, exactly.

Wayne: So let's talk about how we gather the right team members, and how do we know when it's time to cut loose the team members that aren't really contributing. Our topics here are onboarding and even offboarding. Let's talk about how we hire.

Amy: It's the four major elements: let's hire for the best, let's train for the best, let's coach the best, and when it's stinky, let it go.

Wayne: There you go.

Amy: It comes down to being able to do all four of those that creates the healthiest culture that celebrates followers, because the team will always judge you by the way you handle the weakest link. So, going back to hiring, I always remember the good Star-Kist commercial, "only the best tasting tuna get to be Star-Kist."

Wayne: Yep.

Amy: A great leader knows what they're fishing for. If you want catfish, then you're ad may be as ridiculously low barred as, *"Are you breathing and do you live within a five mile radius and you're willing to take the least amount of money?"* And with an ad like that...You're going to get a catfish, a bottom-feeder. If you want tuna, you better know how to fish for tuna.

Wayne: Exactly. Years ago, I got to see Tom Peters *(In Search of Excellence)* speak, and one of the things he talked about was "Hire Talent" — that there are skills that can be taught, that very specific *skills* can be taught.

 **NUCKIN' FUTZ NUGGET:** Hire talent and treat that talent well, because when someone is great with people, for example, that's something that usually cannot be taught. But they can be taught to answer the phone in a certain way, they can be taught to greet your clientele in a certain way.

Amy: I have a very recent Nuckin' Futz. Leadership Lesson on this one.

Wayne: We love those.

Amy: We're going to change the name to protect the guilty. We're going to pretend this particular doctor is named Dr. Pineapple. Dr. Pineapple was really struggling with hiring a new team member. It had been going on for months with the constant complaint that, well, unemployment is almost at zero percent, nobody really needs a job and there's no talent.

So, I was actually in the office, and we had re-written the ad for Indeed.com. I said, "I'm going to review and sort the resumes." I found about five A's, three B's and a partridge in a pear tree. When I asked the doctor whether they were A's, B's, or C's, the doctor saw them all as C's. That's number one. Number two, I then called my A's, and as opposed to scheduling them, my screening for the phone call was very wide and broad, and if they showed any signs of life, we brought them in. And we didn't wait to put them in the schedule two weeks from now—I actually brought somebody in that very day. I then watched the team's interview process, and the first five questions were: Do you understand what the commute is? Where do you live? What happens if you're spending an hour in traffic? And that's not hiring for attitude, aptitude or meaning.

Wayne: No, that's not even close to any kind of talent that's needed internally.

Amy: Exactly. It then turned out that this person was actually a foreign-trained dentist that did not want to get credentialed and wanted to be chair-side, and the doctor's response was, "I would never hire a foreign dentist because they may be arrogant and tell me how to do my dentistry." Long story short, Dr. Pineapple had every, every obstacle, barrier, in the way of ever actually seeing the potential talent in front of them. He was hiring to avoid obstacles versus hiring to hire the best. Obviously, I whipped him into shape and hopefully, most of those obstacles will be removed, and they will be hiring very soon.

Wayne: That's great. So, when you hire the right person, then it's a matter of, "Just tell 'em to go do their job."

No! That can't be the way. So you hire the right person, and you have to tell them what your expectations are *and train them*. There's that magic phrase, "Train them." Train them to actually do the job that they were hired to do.

Amy: And that training requires a great deal of direction and a great deal of support, while they eat the elephant one bite at a time. There's nothing worse than hiring, and then throwing that brand new tuna into the shark-infested waters saying, "Here's my training, I want you to work." And they ask, "How?" And you say, "Hard. I want you to schedule." "How?" "Full. I want you to do that and then hopefully we never talk again in six months." No, people require structure.

Wayne: And the support part means you are circling back to check on, "where are you finding this easy? Show me how you do it. Where are you having challenges? Show me what the challenges are," and really stepping in and supporting them through the places that are challenging and probably somewhere along the way, acknowledging and giving them a verbal high-five for doing the job correctly.

Amy: Which goes right into the coaching element.

Wayne: Absolutely.

Amy:

NUCKIN' FUTZ NUGGET: You have got to catch your followers in the act of doing things right, almost right, or not completely wrong, and acknowledge it. Hold the mirror up to it—it's not just the praise, the nice gesture. It's, I see this. I value this. It ties to our why, and our how's and our strategy and this is what I expect in the future, because we all know that what gets acknowledged, gets repeated.

In the early learning/doing band, acknowledgement is incredibly important to actually reinforce that new skill into muscle memory so it becomes automatic.

Wayne: So I'll ask our readers— well first I have a statement, then a question: You _do_ get more of what you focus on. How many times have you said, "Oh, try not to do this again." and all of a sudden, that thing that you said, "Don't do this again," about, shows up again. You know, when you focus on, "This is the negative thing, don't do it," I think it really needs to be balanced by, "This is the expectation. This is the outcome. This is the envisioned outcome of this task, let's see you do that. What is it going to take to get closer to that." Your coaching needs to be all about what the end desired result is supposed to look like.

Amy: And you need to be there, when they get there, with a giant, "Yippe-ki-yay!" Otherwise, they're going to lose their way, because even when you delegate, people deserve to feel that they're being acknowledged, appreciated, valued, included and respected. And with that said, Dr. Pride used to have a very weird saying that, "You can put your socks in the oven, but that don't make 'em biscuits." What I mean by that is eventually, if that nice little biscuit smell, actually smells like dirty socks, it may be time to actually screw your courage to the sticking place and let them go. Part of your counseling hat is that if the team is judging you by the way you handle the weakest link, if that weak link is still there 20 years later, you've truly, truly made your culture impossible to actually replicate and move forward and be inspiring. So the kindest thing that you can do as a counselor is to sort the socks out of the biscuits. As we like to say, "Drop kick them through the goalposts of life" in the nicest, and kindest and clearest way possible.

Wayne: I think this bears going into a little bit deeper, because sometimes as leaders, we don't want to hurt other people's feelings.

Amy: Yes.

Wayne: What that does is it drags the whole team down. That feeling of, "I can't let them go because they have this or that going on in their personal life. I can't let them go because I said we'd invest in them just that bit more." And the truth is, when you actually get to the place of having counseled them, having realized that they can't do what you are asking them to do, you do need to let them go. It is like cutting an anchor from a boat that has been trying to set sail for a very long time. You will watch your team, the remaining team members, pull together and say, "(sigh) Captain... finally! You actually cut it loose." They'll be relieved, they'll be grateful, and they will pull together in a way that you haven't seen happen in a long time. This is a thing that you need to do, as much as you may dread letting someone go, there are times where that is the best thing for the practice, the best thing for the business, the best thing for you as an individual, and surprisingly, the best thing for the person you're letting go.

Amy: It's a kick in the head, right.

Wayne: In a very positive way. It's a wake-up call. But also, what I found in doing some exit-interviews with people is that it's been a relief in some ways. They have been hiding, hoping not to be "found out." There are team members that are waiting to be let go because they knew they couldn't do the job, and so they've been carrying the burden of, "One more day, I hope I don't mess up." By you letting them go, you've saved them the trouble of having to have the courage to actually admit that.

Amy: There is no rationale under the sun, moon and stars to accept non-performance for the long-haul.

Wayne: Right.

Amy: From any of your talent. If you want to quote a sports analogy, when a performer can no longer perform, when an athlete can no longer do what is expected, they can no longer be part of the team; and you're absolutely right, it can be done with direction, with support. It doesn't have to be judgmental, or mean. We're referring to assertive communication which we talked about earlier. The faster you pull that band-aid off the wound, the better off the individual who is leaving is going to be, the better off you're going to be, and the better off your followers are going to be.

Wayne: So. I have a couple of examples that overlap, and they have to do with an impaired employee. In both cases, the employee showed up looking like she was on drugs or some kind of medication. It is really important that you recognize a couple of things: one is questioning whether that person is fit for duty. Can they do the job that they're hired to do? That's a huge question because whether or not they're sleep deprived, whether or not they're on meds, whether or not they're on legal or illegal drugs, that's really not your judgment to make. What you need to focus on is whether they can do the job that they're hired to do. Did you coach them enough to give them what they needed to do, to do their job? And if they show that they just can't do their job, then it's time to say, "I have asked you to do x. You have shown me y, and I still need x."

Amy: Very clearly, this is what we need to fulfill our vision, our strategy, and our goals. This is what has been demonstrated over a period of time. This can no longer continue. I thank you for your contribution up to this point, and it ends today.

Wayne: Right, I think it's important to note that we're talking about specific behaviors. So when you've had a conversation with any of your team members, you're saying that this behavior has appeared here or this behavior has not appeared here. Not, you look tired, you look stoned, you look like you can't do your job, you look angry. Talk about the behavior or the outcome that you expected.

What is the behavior that's being demonstrated and what is the result of that behavior? One quick example is when someone was impaired, and it was a combination of both medicine and sleep deprivation. The employee actually laughed when a patient made a comment that was very distressing about something that had happened at home. When an inappropriate reaction happens from an employee, it causes that patient or client (your customer) to feel like they're being judged. The outcome is that you could lose that person's business. So the action path you need to follow is to first, document that the behavior was inappropriate, and what the behavior was. Then note what the response was. You'll also need to point out that the outcome of losing customers could actually end up being a huge detriment to the business.

Work Harder

When you have that perspective, it makes the letting go easier. You have to be able to document what it was, what you've done to support, what you saw, and as you said, Amy, that it ends today.

Amy: And never forget that in order for the balance of nature to work at all, as much as you love your team—and trust me I love my team and I even love your teams. I don't know your teams but I love your teams—

Wayne: So do I...!

Amy: **NUCKIN' FUTZ NUGGET: For the balance of nature to work at all, an individual team member, or follower, needs to want their job just a "milli-skosh" more than you want them in their job.** And a "milli-skosh" is a really tiny "skosh." It's less than a milliliter, right? What we mean by that is, if you're feeling you're held hostage by a non-performing staff member, you will never build a culture of enrolled followers, who are inspired by your vision and want to do what you want them to do! And that's the secret of the culture, of creative followership.

Wayne: Exactly. Good stuff!

CHAPTER 5

So What - Now What?

Amy: You know what drives me bat crazy, Wayne, about reading books about leadership?

Wayne: What Amy? What?

Amy: Mostly by the time I get to the final chapter it's like, "Okay, and what do I do now?"

Wayne: Right, you're left with no real action plan or map.

Amy: Exactly because "...it's either all ethereal and intangible and sounds great on paper, but you don't know my team, or it's just so thoroughly overwhelming and I am in the deep depths of despair and *sucktitude* that I see no way to actually take that first step and actually create a culture that I can be proud of." So it would really, really be horrible if anyone who took the time to actually read and learn from our Leadership Lessons From The Road, couldn't walk away with something that they could do tomorrow to actually improve their leadership, create a better culture, inspire a little bit more team success, excitement, yada, yada, yada.

Wayne: Exactly. And I'm hoping, Dear Reader, that you might have been taking notes, because one of the things I like to do is to pose a challenge to make a list of the things that you need to do with your team. Also, Amy and I are going to be pushing you here to do a few things: We want you to do some reflection and then take some action. We've got some pretty great ideas in mind for you (but it requires some action on your part).

Amy: Yeah. You know it's interesting because my method to consulting, training, coaching, and running my own business myself is choose your battles wisely. I always break those battles into what I refer to as sudden impact, or immediate impact. What's the one thing that I can do immediately to decrease stress and increase efficiency enough to get to number two.

Wayne: Right. You need to take action on what's called "the needle movers." What makes the most impact right now. Don't just go for the low hanging fruit. Really, invest in yourself by focusing on your leadership. What do you need to be doing right now to make the biggest impact? And this isn't about putting out fires.

Amy: Now if you only do that, then you're going to be a reactive crisis leader for the rest of your life. You do the sudden impact quickies so that you can get to the long-term implementation steps that actually are the things that change the culture and move the needle.

Wayne: And I would advise our readers, also, tha
it's not taking action. Sometimes the "a‹
to stop doing something. Here are some quesᴜᴏ..
for you to consider as we get into this: What are you
going to start doing? What are you going to stop
doing? What are you going to do more of? What are
you going to do less of?

Amy: And I would add, and what do you think your
culture is going to look like, feel like, or sound like as
a result of those first four questions?

Wayne: Right. That brings me back to our first action step, at
least to my mind, which is <u>let's review your Vision</u>.
Go back, take a look at your vision. What is it? Do
you *own* it? Is it clear? Have you been talking about
it? Have you been talking about it with your team?
Have you been talking about it with your patients/
clientele? They need to feel it, too! So really when
it comes to your vision, the question is, *How are you
developing your culture around it?*

Amy: The next thing I would do is involve your team.
We've already talked about not being the wizard of
Oz behind the curtain, being the leader in a vacuum.
I think that one of the most courageous things a
leader can do is to ask for input from the team. "I
read a book, I had my ideas on what I could do as
a leader to improve, but it takes two to tango, and
what do you need from me, what would you like
to see change?" Those very same questions can be

answered as a dialogue versus the monologue so that you and your team are walking together on the journey towards excellent leadership and excellent followership.

Wayne: Agreed. This is where all of the previous chapters start to come together. You are making it happen when you start with Vision and walk your way toward excellent leadership AND excellent followership.

Amy: There you go. Now the other point is, again, Rome wasn't built in a day. You have to give yourself the grace and dignity to understand that cultures don't change on a dime. It's the oil tanker. It takes three miles to start, and three miles to stop. So give yourself some time. Review the Nuckin' Futz Nuggets. In fact, in the up and coming pages, we are capturing all of our Nuckin' Futz Nuggets. It's a Nuckin' Futz jamboree!

Wayne: It is a Nuckin' Futz jamboree! It's so great that you, our dear reader, have been on this journey with us. Check out the resource section we have in the section following this one and be sure to go to www. NuckinFutz.com to download a copy of them, as well.

Amy: What I highly recommend that you do is that you break down those Nuggets to which ones you will act on and in what order: these are urgent nuggets, these are important nuggets, these are nice to know but something we can focus on in the future. It is absolutely essential that one looks at themselves, looks at their team, and looks at their outcomes with gradient levels of success and change built in.

Wayne: Yeah Amy, think of it as a grid: Look at yourself, look at your team, look at your desired outcomes. Those are huge categories, they're huge buckets into which your tasks fall. Make sure that you're really paying attention to how the vision, how your communication, and for all of those things that we've talked about as you read through the nuggets, make sure you're paying attention to how those weave through each of those categories.

Amy: You know Wayne it's important, and I think that one of the most important points as we help people continue on their journey to being better and more effective leadership is to realize you're not isolated in the sticky dark alone.

Wayne: Too true. You are not alone. So many have come before you. So many will come after.

Amy: Yes, the reason we've shared the stories in this book is because we all are on the journey. We all have walked the walk and talked the talk, and sometimes not walked or talked. All of us have been, from time to time, Nuckin' Futz. This is not a journey we want you making alone. This is gather together and realize that it does take courage to be a leader, and others have walked the path and done it with success. Learn from them, do from them. Remember that the book is the event, not the process. There is a website that we've created to inspire a Nuckin' Futz community that I'm very excited about.

Wayne: You'll have some resources available. All of the Nuckin' Futz nuggets will be there for you to download. We'll have other surprises there too. That is all at www.NuckinFutz.com.

Amy: In the words of our fearless leader, Dr. Jim Pride, "When I accepted my role as a leader, I started sleeping like a baby. Which means I woke up every two hours wet and crying for my mommy." Yes, indeed, it's a "Depends moment." But what I'm hoping is that we've shared some effective ways to wake up every now and then a little less wet and a little more hopeful.

Wayne: Absolutely. Waking up in gratitude is a really great place to start. I would offer that as a way to transform any lingering anxiety into something that you're really happy and grateful about. Today, you get to make your difference as a leader. Today, you get to serve. Will that exact a toll on you? Certainly. So is it going to be work? Yes! Is it something I'm grateful for? Yes!

Amy: Congratulations, and go ye forth and multiply your inspiration, your passion, and excitement as you continue to learn Leadership Lessons From The Road. Yippee ki-yay! Rock and roll!

With gratitude to you, Dear Reader – Dear Leader, as you take on another day. Go on and look at what we have for you at www.NuckinFutz.com.

NUCKIN' FUTZ NUGGETS

Available as a download at
www.NuckinFutz.com

 Take a moment and think about this: What's your big why? What gets you out of bed in the morning? And then, lock that in a little bit. Every leader and every individual within a team needs to understand what their personal vision is, to see how it aligns with what the company's vision is and be able to truly say "I believe in that!"

 These three words—inspirational, aspirational and perspirational—are about building on the foundation that moves your business forward. Your vision does serve to be *inspirational*; it serves to breathe life back into your plan, your true desires, which are values based, by the way. Then *aspirational*, that you're moving toward something bigger, grander than what you have and are right now. And the *perspirational* part is that there is work to be done to move toward that North Star.

 It's not a burden if it actually is a North Star that you truly desire. The perspiration is worth it if you desire it.

Although the vision should be a unifier for a business, the true purpose of the vision statement is to be the "mothership," Synergy comes from finding team members who have a personal vision and who view the mothership as a vehicle to accomplish their own vision. Win-Win!

Yes, we now all agree that the Why is almighty, all powerful. It is the plug that holds your business' bathtub water in. But without the How, it's empty rhetoric.

Rate yourself on the vision at the end of the day. On a scale of 1 to 10, did I live into it? Did I do this thing I said I'd do? Did I do *this* thing I said I'd do? Did I do <u>this</u> thing I said I would do?

The vision acts as the lens through which all decisions are made. And that means action is taken only when filtered by asking, "does this match our vision?"

Remember that <u>*you can't give what you don't have*</u>. When you've run out of fuel because you've given everything you have, there's nothing left to give.

Going all the way back to your vision being a filter, as the third person in the room with you, to base your successful culture on the vision: You need to use it to catch your patients/clients and your team doing things right, almost right, or not completely wrong, and acknowledge it. Appreciate it, value it, and grow the company's culture, your team members, and their behavior through the inspiring lens of the vision.

They have to hear your voice. They have to hear it. They have to watch your skin tone. They have to notice the inflection and even your breathing. They need to see your authentic excitement or enthusiasm.

If it feels dead, Dear Leader, that's you. And that means that you have to really reflect on the energy that you're putting into your Vision and bringing to the team.

Focus on answering this: What are we communicating and why?

It is essential for any leader of a team—large or small—to become comfortable with assertive communication! "Here's what I see, this is what I need, and what are your next steps to achieve a positive outcome?"

It is important to understand the differences between "push communication" versus "pull communication." There are times when you have information that must be disseminated quickly via "push communication" you'll push it out, spit it out, do it, and get the information that everybody needs out there. The problem is that there's no guarantee of it being heard as intended. So really, the remedy is to pull. Practice "pull" Communication, where you're asking questions to gain understanding and buy-in. (This is also known as the Socratic Method of teaching.)

 People buy into what they have helped create!

 Under-communication demands a return back to your values and what's reflected in the vision. What part of the vision or what part of the values are not being carried forward?

 What you *think* you're saying very often is not heard the way in which you would like it to be heard. Pay attention to the responses. (Go back to "pull" for understanding.)

 Be careful when you triangulate and start that good old telephone game, because you might start by saying "you have failed in this particular task," and in translation it might sound like "you're fired." This will not address the change you desire!

 Leadership is perception. It has absolutely nothing to do with what you said. It has everything to do with how it's perceived.

 Leadership is all about perception.

Credibility. Flexibility. Congruence. These are not a one-and-done kind of thing. These are communicated in *every* moment. The whole idea about congruence is, are you living into your best self? *Are you modeling the way?*

Your team will not trust you, or trust your leadership, if you're not willing to get your hands dirty.

 Make use of the feedback along the way while keeping the specific end result in mind!

 As a leader, you choose your style and, like any art, it is crafted a day at a time. Keep honing.

 The wisest leader knows how much direction is needed, how much support is needed, and that when you blend them correctly, you get "motion in your ocean."

 If you are not getting the *perceived* change or *perceived* movement that you want, <u>*your*</u> perception counts as the leader. Redirect. Communicate differently.

 Every team member deserves to have coaching and counseling where appropriate. They deserve it, and as a leader it's your duty to actually provide it.

 Your team will love black and white parameters as long as they are wide and thoroughly communicated.

 If you can't measure it, then you can't counsel to it. If you can't measure it, you can't coach to it.

 Followers don't have to be sheep—followers can be dynamic and can be engaged as worker bees. They can be invested team leaders; however, the follower *chooses* to follow.

Creating true followers means that you are being clear about your expectations.

One of the things that is a common mistake is that delegation cannot occur until there is mutually agreed upon, demonstrated, consistent mastery of the job, the task, or the skill.

Not everybody is supposed to be first-string, but first-string can't be effective, unless there's an equally effective second-string right behind them, to be able to keep the game going, to keep the momentum going.

Delegating to someone who barely wants to show up to do their job is a really bad idea.

The meeting is the place to talk about expectations.

It is very important to clarify the purpose and the expected outcomes of the meeting.

Hire talent and treat that talent well, like someone who is great with people, for example, because that's something that usually cannot be taught.

You have got to catch your followers in the act of doing things right, almost right, or not completely wrong, and acknowledge what you've seen.

For the balance of nature to work at all, an individual team member, or follower, needs to want their job just a "milli-skosh" more than *you* want them in their job.

 Leadership is a constant process that requires commitment. Keep learning. Keep investing in yourself, and keep investing in your team.

 YOU are a leader! Find moments for which you are grateful. What you are leading is greater than yourself and provides the ability to serve.

Thank you for joining us on our journey of Leadership Lessons From The Road.

We might all be a little Nuckin' Futz, but that is part of what keeps it interesting!

Remember to reach out to us and find more resources at

www.NuckinFutz.com

AUTHORS' BIOGRAPHIES

Amy Morgan is a renowned consultant, trainer who has been inspiring success in small business's for over 25 years (yes, per Amy, she's old!). As CEO of Pride Institute, Amy and her team have revitalized thousands of dental practices using Pride's time-proven Management Systems, with the goal of those business's becoming more efficient and profitable, with less stress (and a great deal more happiness).

Amy is no stranger to writing though this (#1 Best-Seller) is her first offering for the general public. She has written volumes of training materials, articles and white papers for team leaders, managers, and business owners, collaborating with Ken Blanchard and the Tom Peters group. With a voice that is unique for its humor, creative language and approachability, Amy has a way of cutting through egos, blame, and judgment in order to inspire change and growth.

Amy is a highly-sought speaker at symposia and universities across the country. In addition, her work has jumped continents as she coaches leaders around the world and lectures internationally from the U.S. and Canada all the way to Scandinavia.

She started her career as a consultant, focusing on the drama of medical and dental practice owners who failed to pay attention to their finances, their statistics, and their cash flow. She became a cash-crisis-consultant, helping small businesses of all sizes shapes and colors, turn their downward spiral into a positive upward trajectory. At that time, Amy realized that statistics by themselves, would never proactively change a culture or insure profitability. Only through leadership, management and organized systems, could businesses steer clear of crisis and achieve long-term success,

Amy's passion for leadership and positively impacting the lives of all she touches has continued (with a little inspiration from her training at Disney☺).

At home in the wine country she scrambles after her two cats - Dave and Kung-Fu Panda Bear Kitty, her husband Geoff (who is her life-long partner in everything she accomplishes), and her two amazing daughters - Becca and Cate, each making their way in the world (inspired by the leadership lessons they have learned from both of their parents).

And of course - living in Sonoma County - Amy's motto is, if you can't solve the problems of your business, there is a bottle of wine with your name on it that may be able to help! (It certainly can't hurt.)

To reach out to Amy, please use the **Contact** field at

www.NuckinFutz.com

As an International #1 Best-Selling author, speaker, and high-performance leadership coach, **Dr Wayne Pernell** is known for helping his clients break through to their next level of success and fulfillment. He is highly sought for speaking, training, and exclusive 1:1 coaching having been in Forbes Magazine and on Fox and NBC morning Television. He founded the DynamicLeader® programs and his work with senior leaders along with his thought-provoking and inspiring previous four books on communication, relationships, and leadership have landed him with the moniker of "the leaders' leader."

After earning his doctorate in clinical psychology, Dr. Pernell began working with organizational leaders and their teams. He has helped guide the leadership in several high-profile companies including Schwab, 3Com, Whole Foods Market, and AAA. Having grown up as the son of a dentist, Dr Pernell circled back to help dental professionals become better leaders. He has been with Pride Institute, a practice management consulting firm based just north of the Golden Gate Bridge in Marin County, since 2005 and now, as the Director of Organization Development and a Senior Consultant, he continues to focus on leadership development, helping his clients to break through to even greater successes.

Also in his background, Dr. Pernell is an accomplished magician, having performed to the amazement and delight of audiences of all ages. While not actually performing magic any more, you're likely to see something magical in everything he does. And yes, there's more. He's a fourth-degree black belt in the multi-disciplinary martial art of Bushido, the *Way* of the Warrior. For three decades, he taught students to continually assess and access available options to best cut through or eliminate conflict. Drawing on these concepts, Sensei Wayne helps his clients get through tough spots by emphasizing the powers of awareness and choice, even during extremely high-pressure situations.

"Dr P," as he's known by his clients and friends, currently resides in the San Francisco Bay Area. Given the chance, he will talk about his wife and kids (three of his own and two bonus daughters) and he notes that they'll call upon him for advice and counsel, an honor he cannot ignore.

Known for being authentic, insightful, and playful, his clients regularly provide accolades such as, "…thank you for the gift of being able to take control of my life" and "This work was life changing." Dr P invites everyone to take advantage of free weekly inspirational and thought-provoking content in his Wednesdays With Wayne, to dive into any of his books, to take his online courses, or to attend one of his Stuck At The Top™ retreats. Those who are all-in may step up for 1:1 advising. Reach out to Dr Wayne Pernell at www.DynamicLeader.com as he continues to achieve break-through levels of personal and professional success.

Dr Wayne Pernell can also be found on all social media outlets and can be contacted via the Nuckin' Futz website at

www.NuckinFutz.com

FREE Downloads And Other Fun Stuff

Available At

www.NuckinFutz.com